STRATEGIES FOR STUDYING

STRATEGIES for STUDYING

A HANDBOOK OF STUDY SKILLS

ORCA BOOK PUBLISHERS

Copyright © 1996 University of Victoria

Canadian Cataloguing in Publication Data
Main entry under title:
Strategies for studying

ISBN 1-55143-063-0
1. Study skills.
LB2395.S86 1996   378.1'7'02812   C96–910474–X

Cover design by Jim Brennan
Printed and bound in Canada

Orca Book Publishers
PO Box 5626, Station B
Victoria, BC   V8R 6S4
Canada

Orca Book Publishers
PO Box 468
Custer, WA 98240-0468
USA

10   9   8   7   6   5   4   3   2   1

Acknowledgements

The first edition of this handbook was based on the Learning Skills Program offered through the University of Victoria's Counselling Services; it was written and revised by members and former members of that program. Sandi Clay was the primary author of the first draft, with Anne Forester as consultant. Dr. J. Parsons, Coordinator of the Learning Skills Program, did the major revisions in consultation with Dr. H. Beach, Director of the Counselling Services. Dr. Martin and Dr. Cochran, former coordinators of the Learning Skills Program, contributed significantly with ideas, material, and exercises that they developed during their tenure in Counselling Services, as did the teaching assistants who have worked in the program. The several thousand students who have taken the Learning Skills Program at the University of Victoria have done much to make the principles and methods of learning described in this handbook practicable and effective.

The first edition of the *Strategies* was designed, coordinated, and produced under the direction of Kate Seaborne, manager of Distance Education Services, Division of Continuing Studies at the University of Victoria.

This second edition of *Strategies* was edited from the original by Geri Rowlatt and the staff of Distance Education Services, Division of Continuing Studies at the University of Victoria. Additional resources in this edition were contributed by the staff of University of Victoria's Counselling Services.

This handbook is designed for all students who want to make the most of their courses. As an adult learner, you likely have many responsibilities — work, family, studies — and only a limited amount of time for studying and learning. But whether you're a first-time or a returning student, you'll find useful information and skills in this handbook to help you become a more efficient and effective learner.

The handbook has several purposes:

- to ease the transition to college and university learning
- to improve existing studying and learning skills
- to develop essay-writing skills
- to increase learning efficiency and productivity
- to reduce wasted time and effort
- to help develop a balanced lifestyle

Although some of the ideas and methods found in this handbook are drawn from the research literature on learning, most are based on the authors' experiences and research work with hundreds of students. What is most important, though, is that you try the studying and learning techniques found throughout the book. Only you can judge whether a particular technique works for you. We hope you'll read about the methods and then select and use what fits your particular learning situation.

CONTENTS

4   WRITING ESSAYS AND REPORTS ... 75

1
What's Involved in Learning?

I. HOW TO USE THIS HANDBOOK

Changing studying and learning habits takes dedication, practice, and rewards. Simply reading about studying and learning techniques won't get you many results, though, which is why this handbook is designed to do more than just tell you how to learn. A number of exercises are included in each section for you to practice the techniques.

 EXERCISE 1: What's Involved in Learning
(10 minutes)

For this exercise, you'll need a pen or pencil, some paper, and a watch or timer.

Do each step before looking ahead.

1. Imagine that you have been asked to serve on the Canadian Fine Arts Committee. The committee's goal is to design a learning/training program for the nation's artists that will produce excellence (and awards).

2. Use 2 minutes to write down all the things an artist should do to become an award winner. Just write all the key words and phrases that come to mind. Do this now and set your imagination free. Here are two suggestions to get you started:

    • practice on a regular basis

    • set goals and subgoals

3. Now, think of a particular fine arts activity (painting, drawing, sculpture, music, theater, etc.) and add some more items to your list. If you run out of ideas, switch to another activity. Take another 2 minutes to build your specific fine art. Do this now.

4. Now take 2 more minutes and review your list of items. Fill in any more details that come to mind. Think about breaking some big items into smaller parts, and as you go over your list, you may get a few more ideas. Do this now.

We've listed our ideas — which took more than 6 minutes to think of — below. How does your list compare to ours?

Things an Artist Should do to Win an Award

Set goals and subgoals

Practice, practice . . .

Set priorities

Get good teachers

Check progress

Take short breaks

Compete/cooperate

Get financial support

Live a balanced life

Relax

Get plenty of rest

Eat nutritious foods

Make sacrifices

Work on technique

Establish a schedule

Notice improvements

Work gradually toward goals

Seek moral support

Observe others

What do you think of this list? Would doing these things help someone become an award-winning artist? Probably.

Of course, these things would also help someone become a good student. Learning involves doing, no matter what you're trying to learn. And that's the real point here. If you want to improve your study and learning skills, you have to do more than just learn about the methods — you have to act (set goals and priorities, practice, etc.).

Other Considerations to Keep in Mind While Using
This Handbook

Just as becoming an award-winning artist requires time and effort, studying and learning habits don't change overnight. A gradual, progressive change works best and stays with you longer.

Some of the techniques in this handbook will work well for you and others won't. But give them all a try and then decide which ones you like.

Try the following general strategy:

- assess your needs using the survey at the beginning of each section
- read about the methods that fit your needs
- do the exercises as you go
- use new methods gradually and progressively
- evaluate each new method and apply it, as you can, to new situations
- reward yourself often for progress

II.   A QUICK OVERVIEW OF THE HANDBOOK

The information in this handbook can be used in two ways. You can "begin at the beginning" and work systematically through each unit as it's presented, or you can "jump around" and work on skills you think you really need to improve. If you haven't already started your course, you may find it useful to go straight through. If you have started, you may want to work selectively with the material.

The next exercise will give you a quick overview of the information and methods found in this handbook. It will also demonstrate a useful reading skill you can begin to use.

Exercise 2: Surveying the Handbook
(20 minutes)

Don't spend more than 20 minutes on this exercise—the aim is to get a good idea of the handbook's contents in a short period of time. You'll need a pen or pencil, some paper, a watch or timer, and two bookmarks (slips of paper will do).

1. Mark this page with one of the bookmarks. Then turn to the Contents page and put the other bookmark there.

2. Use 1 minute to study the titles in the Contents for Sections 2 through 5, with the intention of remembering them in your own words. Do this now.

3. Next, without looking at the Contents page, write the section titles from memory on your paper. Don't worry about the order. Do this now.

4. Next, for Section 2: Managing Time Effectively, read the major headings (the headings with Roman numerals). As you read, think about what might be covered under each heading. Take 2 minutes to do Section 2. Do this now.

5. Now, without looking, write the major headings of Section 2 from memory on your paper. Check the Contents page to see if you remembered all of them. Do this now.

6. Return to the Contents (Section 2) and read the subheadings. Consider how each one relates to its major heading and the section title. Do this now.

7. Then, write one short paragraph summarizing Section 2, without looking back. Do this now.

    The "survey" exercise you just did for Section 2 is the first step to take when preparing to read a chapter of any book. This is how you learn the basic structure of information within the chapter and some of the main concepts that will be covered.

8. Take what remains of the 20 minutes to practice this skill with the other sections. Do each section as fast as you can. Do this now.

Now that you've surveyed each section, you should have a good idea of what's in this handbook and how it's organized. For example, you probably noticed that "surveying" is covered in detail in Section 3: Reading and Remembering.

Have you reached your "saturation point" yet? That's the point at which you're unlikely to absorb any more detail and need to take a break and relax for a few minutes. When you study, taking short breaks can be an effective technique to improve your learning.

III. IMPLEMENTING SKILLS

It's important to apply the studying and learning techniques to your actual course materials as soon as possible.

 Exercise 3: Implementing Skills (5 minutes)

Try using the chapter survey technique you just learned with a chapter from your own textbook. Take 5 minutes at most and do this now.

Now you're ready to work with the rest of the handbook. Whether you're going to work straight through it or with particular sections, spend 45 to 60 minutes working on some part of the handbook. After trying the exercises, you can then use the methods you've learned on your own course materials.

2
Managing Time Effectively

Survey Your Present Habits

		Always	Almost Always	Usually	Sometimes	Almost Never	Never
1	I have enough time to do all that I need to do.						
2	I have enough time to do all that I want to do.						
3	I set realistic goals for each day for what I want to get done.						
4	I make a list each day of the things I want and need to do.						
5	I set priorities each day, noting things I must do, things I could do, and things I could put off.						
6	I have a weekly plan with time set aside for work, studies, and social/leisure activities.						
7	I can concentrate when studying for long time periods (e.g., 1 hour) without being distracted or daydreaming.						
8	I'm highly motivated to do my daily activities.						
9	I use my time wisely and seldom delay doing things.						
10	I make wise use of small blocks of time (5 to 15 minutes).						
11	I could account for at least 90% of my time (e.g., yesterday).						

If you answered "sometimes," "almost never," or "never" to most of these survey items, you might benefit from the exercises in this section.

"Procrastination is my middle name."
"I'd love to go, but I just can't find the time."
"Once I get started I'm okay, but I just can't get started."

Do these comments sound familiar? If so, you've got lots of company. Few of us seem to have enough time these days. But even though you can't add more hours to your day, you can learn to use the hours you do have more effectively. The next section will help you do this.

I.   HOW DO I SPEND MY TIME NOW?

Before you can really learn how to make your time work for you, you need to think about how you spend and use your time right now.

 Exercise 1: Increasing Awareness

The first step toward using your time more effectively is becoming aware of your current activities, the demands on your time, and how you spend your time. This awareness process is like financial planning and following a budget, but the payoffs can be even better.

1. For this exercise, you keep a journal of your activities for one complete day. Remove one of the following Time-Monitoring Form sheets.

2. Now, look at the sample that follows. It's filled in to show the starting time, ending time, and the amount of time used for each activity throughout the day.

3. If tomorrow is a typical day, use the Time-Monitoring Form to record your activities and time use. If you forget to fill in something when you do it, write it in later as best you can. But this process works best if you have the form with you and fill it in as the day passes.

A sample time-monitoring form for late afternoon might look something like this.

Start	End	Time Used	Activity Description	Rating 1 = Poor 5 = Great	Analysis
4:30	4:45	15 min.	drive home from work		
4:45	5:30	45 min.	read paper and watch a game show on TV		
5:30	6:30	60 min.	cook and eat dinner		
6:30	7:30	60 min.	listen to stereo and study		
7:30	7:45	15 min.	phone friend long distance		

4. When you finish an activity, rate the time you spent according to how productive or useful it was to you. Give yourself a "1" if the time was wasted and a "5" if the time was very useful and fulfilling. Give yourself a "2," "3," or "4" if the time spent fell somewhere between Poor and Great.

5. After recording your activities for one full day, take a close look at your entries. Could you have used your time more effectively? Jot down your thoughts in the Analysis column (see following sample).

Start	End	Time Used	Activity Description	Rating 1 = Poor 5 = Great	Analysis
4:30	4:45	15 min.	drive home from work	3	can't change time spent
4:45	5:30	45 min.	read paper and watch a game show on TV	4	relaxation time O.K.
5:30	6:30	60 min.	cook and eat dinner	3	O.K., but maybe we could've had a better dinner conversation
6:30	7:30	60 min.	listen to stereo and study	2	it's hard to concentrate when listening to stereo. Choice too demanding.
7:30	7:45	15 min.	phone friend long distance	5	save this for a reward for later!

6. Finally, reflect upon each entry. How important is it to you and your goals? Could your time be better spent?

A. USING TIME MONITORING TO INCREASE EFFICIENCY

You may find that keeping track of your time in this way helps you to be more efficient, or be more goal-directed, or lead a more balanced life. If that's the case, you now have a method of managing your time better and for being more productive.

Time-Monitoring Form

Time		Time Used	Activity Description	Rating 1 = Poor 5 = Great	Analysis
Start	End				

Time-Monitoring Form

Time		Time Used	Activity Description	Rating 1 = Poor 5 = Great	Analysis
Start	End				

II.   GOALS AND PLANS

A. DECIDING WHAT'S IMPORTANT

Many people find themselves overwhelmed with the number of things they need to do each day. Sometimes we get so confused and frustrated, we don't do anything. That's why it's important to decide what you really need to do and then schedule enough time to get it done. Remember that the purpose of planning is to help you gain control of your time and take charge of your life.

The first step is deciding what you really need to get done. For example, a To-Do List for a part-time student might look like this on any given day of the week.

1.   Do laundry
2.   Read chapter of textbook
3.   Choose essay topic for paper
4.   Phone Neil
5.   Write two letters
6.   Make dentist appointment
7.   Spend time with the kids

Exercise 2: Daily Plans (5 minutes)

1. Take time now to make a To-Do List of all the specific things you'd like to get done tomorrow.

    _____

    _____

    _____

    _____

    _____

    _____

    _____

2. Now, beside each item place one of the following letters:

    A — for what must be done tomorrow

    B — for what should be done or you'd like to get done

    C — for what can easily be postponed a day or two

3. After you've done this, look at your B items. Place these into either the A list or the C list.

4. Now, transfer your top-priority tasks (your A's) onto a slip of paper or a small, easily carried notepad.

5. As the day goes by, refer to your list and complete your A tasks as you can, crossing off each one as soon as it's done.

Many people write their To-Do List for tomorrow's tasks at the end of each day, as this eliminates lying in bed worrying about forgetting to do something. Remember to cross off each task as you do it.

Exercise 3: Using a Daily To-Do List
(10 minutes)

On each day for a full week, make up a To-Do List of top-priority goals. At the end of the week, decide whether the To-Do Lists have helped you. Don't be surprised or frustrated if you don't accomplish every goal each day — 80% is very good.

You can keep track on this form now and later use a calendar.

	Day 1	Day 2	Day 3	Day 4	Day 5	Day 6	Day 7	Total
Number of A goals set								
Number of A goals finished								

B. SETTING STUDY GOALS

Students will often state their goals like this:

work on essay
study math
read economics text

Goals like these are not very clear, though. After an hour of "studying math," you aren't quite sure whether you've accomplished anything.

So what kind of goals should you set? Your study goals should include these four characteristics:

- **short term** — You should be able to reach your goal in the time limit you've set. Reading 3 or 4 chapters of economics may be too much for one day.

- **specific** — Make your goal specific, that is, something you can get to work on right away. Instead of "studying math," "doing 5 math problems" would make that goal more specific.

- **attainable** — Only you know what your limitations are. It's better to set a goal you know you can achieve in your study time instead of one you think you might or want to achieve. Practice success!

- **measurable** — You should be able to tell at the end of a study session whether you've done what you set out to do. So, use phrases like "make notes on 10 pages of Economics," "write 3 Math formulas from memory," etc.

1. Making Your Goals Work for You

As you go through this handbook, goal-setting will become easier and more efficient. You'll learn to realize and recognize that you can't reach a major goal in a single sitting or even a full day. Here is a procedure you can follow for setting goals.

	Goal-setting Action	Our Example	Write Your Goal Here (It might be doing a reading assignment or an essay.)
1	Pick a major study goal.	2,000-word paper on Economics	
2	Break your goal into steps that fit your goal.	A. Choose topic B. Make outline C. Do research outline D. Write E. Proofread	
3	Break the first step into substeps.	A. Choose topic A.1 Decide on a general area of interest A.2 Brainstorm ideas A.3 Narrow and choose specific topic A.4 Define terms	
4	Select one or more substeps you can complete in your next study hour and do them.	A.1 Choose area of interest A.2 Brainstorm	
5	Reward yourself on completion of goal.	Take a break	
6	Return to #4 and continue as time and circumstances permit.	A.3 Narrow topic A.4 Define terms	

2. Scheduling Study Time

The key to a successful study schedule is a combination of flexibility and discipline. A schedule should allow for unexpected events: new demands at work, a friend dropping over, a dinner invitation, or visitors from out of town. But discipline is the key. Stick to your schedule as much as possible and reschedule — as soon as you can — whatever you didn't get done.

 Exercise 4: Filling Out an Academic Term Calendar (15 minutes)

Two scheduling forms are included in this section. The first one is an Academic Term Calendar. On this sheet (or any other calendar or day planner), mark in assignment due dates and dates when you have to prepare for exams, seminars, or classes. Then, record dates when you know you won't get any work done (e.g., Amanda's wedding). You can now see how much time you have to work on each assignment. Take time to fill in your term calendar now.

To prepare your term calendar:

1. Enter scheduled exams, seminars, holidays, trips, etc.

2. Add assignment due dates as they are given.

3. The term calendar is an easy way to organize your work. Once you know your fixed commitments and have an organized daily and weekly schedule, jotting down daily work on your term calendar will keep you on top of your assignments. During your heaviest and busiest times in the term, you may want to use a detailed daily or weekly schedule in addition to your term calendar.

Academic Term Calendar

Week of	Monday	Tuesday	Wednesday	Thursday	Friday	Saturday	Sunday

Exercise 5: Filling Out a Weekly Time Schedule
(10 minutes)

The other form, the Weekly Time Schedule, is much more detailed than the term calendar. On this schedule, write in everything you do on a regular basis (e.g., classes, work). Next, mark off enough time for meals, including time for preparation, eating, relaxing, and clean-up. Now, check to see how much time is available to you. From this open time, select several hours you can use for studying. The average three-unit university course might require between 10 and 14 hours of study per week; this total includes class time, review, reading, and writing assignments. Can you schedule study time during the day so you can use your evenings for other things?

To prepare your Weekly Time Schedule:

1. Enter non-study activities you do each week (e.g., classes, work, favorite TV programs, chores, etc.).

2. Block off time for meals, sleep, family/social activities, exercise, and recreation.

3. Schedule time for study (say 10 hours per course per week).

4. Stay flexible but determined.

Weekly Time Schedule

Hour	Monday	Tuesday	Wednesday	Thursday	Friday	Saturday	Sunday
7:30							
8:30							
9:30							
10:30							
11:30							
12:30							
1:30							
2:30							
3:30							
4:30							
5:30							
6:30							
7:30							
8:30							
9:30							
10:30							
11:30							

3. Things to Keep in Mind When Scheduling Study Time

- Contrast activities. For example, if you spend two hours studying, allow time for some physical activity afterward.

- Give yourself breaks. A 50-minute hour is a good plan for studying. Study 50 minutes and then take a 10-minute break. Often that 10-minute break will give those new ideas a chance to sink in. Take breaks before you really need them and use them to reward yourself.

- Work when you're most alert. If you're wide awake at 7:00 p.m., don't use that valuable time for doing the laundry or watching TV. Use your wide-awake time for studying.

- Make use of small chunks of time. A 10-minute break can give you time to review notes for a chapter or answer a question for an assignment. A list of 10-minute tasks can reduce wasted decision time.

- Reward yourself for completing goals. Rewards can take many forms: leisure activities (go to a concert), noting accomplishments (tell a friend), tangible rewards (buy something special to make for dinner), or a simple relaxing break (listen to your new CD).

III. STUDY SPOTS AND DEVELOPING CONCENTRATION

A. SETTING ASIDE A STUDY SPOT

Have you ever walked through a college or university campus during exam time and watched students studying? They study (or appear to study) in cafeterias, in hallways, on the grass while soaking up the sun, in noisy classrooms, at bus stops, draped over cushions, and, yes, some even study in the library. Although these areas have their merits — comfort, convenience, friends, sunshine — they do not, with the exception of the library, give you a place to settle down, spread books around you, and get down to work with a minimal number of distractions. The kindest thing you can do for yourself is find one place that you can always use for studying.

Ideally, this study spot should be just yours, a place where you can leave your books and materials even when you're not there. It may be a large walk-in closet that you've converted to a study, a desk in your bedroom, or a corner of your living room. Most important, it should be a place where you'll be as free as possible from distractions, and where you'll feel comfortable studying. Sitting down to study will also be easier if you have good lighting, your books and papers within easy reach, and everything that might take your mind off your work put away. If you don't live alone, you need to ask not to be disturbed when you're in your study spot and to have your phone calls held. In the long run, this will be easier on everyone; if you're constantly interrupted, you may get frustrated and short-tempered.

Think of your regular study spot. Are you in it right now? What else do you do there?

> Eat?
> Balance the checkbook?
> Watch TV?
> Talk to family?
> Use the phone?
> Sleep?
> Daydream?

To increase your concentration and make your study time more effective, teach yourself to only study in your study spot. If you do other things in that spot, they tend to compete for your attention and make it hard for you to concentrate. What you want is a place that encourages studying and learning and nothing else.

B. DEVELOPING CONCENTRATION

Good concentration is necessary for effective and efficient studying. Here are some steps you can take to teach yourself to concentrate better.

1. Use a Study Spot

- Locate a spot that is both free of distractions and you can reserve for study only. If you can't reserve a desk or room, pick a place you don't normally use (e.g., a chair at the kitchen table that you rarely use).

- The next time you're in the mood to study, go there with a small, specific, and reasonable task to do. Prepare the space for work (with paper, dictionary, etc.) and then start.

- If you finish the task, immediately leave that spot and take a short break. Then, repeat the procedure, gradually increasing the amount of work you want to get done in each sitting. The idea is to practice success and build concentration gradually.

Note: Although you probably won't want to stop for a break when you're concentrating well and have finished a task, do it anyway. If you only stop when you can't concentrate any longer and aren't getting much done, you're actually rewarding yourself for poor concentration. Reward yourself for good concentration instead.

2. When You Start to Lose Concentration

If, for whatever reason, you lose concentration before you finish your task:

- decide at once to take a break, or,
- set an immediate small goal (e.g., read one more paragraph, do one more small problem, etc.)
- refocus your attention and complete your small goal
- then take your break

Again, the idea is to reward good concentration. You can improve your productivity by following this concentration training method, but only if you practice it consistently.

3. Other Concentration Tips

- Do distracting thoughts and worries often keep you from studying? If so, keep a notebook on your desk to jot down any thoughts or worries so you can deal with them when you're done studying. At least this way, you won't worry about forgetting them.

- If you have to study in a noisy area (people in the hall, TV in another room, traffic noise) and find you can't concentrate, try listening to music — no lyrics, low volume — while you study. A steady, pleasant sound can cover up a number of other noises.

IV. TIME SAVERS

Here are some helpful time-saving techniques you can try. Use the ones that work for you.

1. Ask your spouse, your children, or your co-workers to take over a few of your responsibilities — the laundry, the yard work, a shift at work, and so on.

2. Show your appreciation to people who help you out.

3. Learn to say "no" when there are too many demands on your time. When you begin to value your time, others will too.

4. Break up a big task into smaller pieces, and do one piece to get started.

5. Put off low-priority tasks and start on high-priority tasks as soon as possible.

6. Make several phone calls in one sitting, when it's convenient for you.

7. Try to handle paperwork only once.

8. Reduce the time you spend on nonproductive or not truly relaxing or enjoyable activities (e.g., watching TV reruns).

9. When reading a textbook, first decide the level of detail you need to learn, and then stop when you achieve it.

10. Use time between major tasks (so-called transition time or waiting time) to do something meaningful. For example, use time spent in a doctor's waiting room to review notes, to make tomorrow's To-Do List, or to just relax.

V.   SUMMARY OF TIME-MANAGEMENT TECHNIQUES

- Take charge of your life. Set goals and achieve them.

- Increase awareness of time use and demands.

- Make plans, schedules, and To-Do Lists as needed.

- Evaluate your goals to make sure they are short term, specific, attainable, and measurable.

- Train yourself to concentrate by practicing and rewarding high concentration.

- Keep track of and use time-management techniques that work for you.

Although anyone can benefit from these techniques, as a student you'll find that by practicing time management, fitting in study time is not only possible but also very rewarding.

VI.   REFERENCES

Refer to Section 6 on page 137 for a complete listing of reference material.

3
Reading and Remembering

Survey Your Present Reading Habits

		Always	Almost Always	Usually	Sometimes	Almost Never	Never
1	I enjoy reading.						
2	I feel that I read well.						
3	I spend more time reading than watching TV.						
4	I know why I'm reading before I start?						
5	I vary my reading speed to suit what I'm reading.						
6	I preview a chapter or book before I read it.						
7	I search for main ideas when I read.						
8	I concentrate on what I'm reading.						
9	I remember what I've read.						
10	I make use of graphs, tables, and pictures while I read.						
11	I practice recalling what I've read.						
12	I take good notes from what I've read.						
13	I organize my notes systematically.						

If you answered "always," "almost always," or "usually" to most of these survey items, you're probably an efficient reader already, and you may just want to skim this section. Otherwise, read over the information and try the exercises.

I.   BEFORE READING FOR DETAIL

Imagine setting out on a journey with only a vague idea of where you're going, how you'll get there, and what you'll find when you arrive — and you only have a limited amount of time. How successful will you be?

Most of us know how to take a physical journey: we plan a route and take a map to avoid getting lost. The steps for taking a thinking journey are less definite, though. You're going into unfamiliar territory where starting on page one of a new textbook and moving along aimlessly are likely to be frustrating and inefficient. What you need is a guideline or a map to keep you on the right track.

A. DETERMINING YOUR PURPOSE

Why are you reading a particular book? Is it to get a general overview of a subject to see if it's worth pursuing, or is this an assigned reading you may be examined on later? Are you reading it to find the answer to a specific question, or are you reading for enjoyment and relaxation?

In order to select the most efficient reading method for a particular book, chapter, or article — and to meet your needs — you must determine your purpose(s). Just a few of the many reasons to read a book are listed here.

Some Possible Reading Purposes

- To pass time
- To get pleasure
- To learn the "gist" of a book
- To determine if the book contains useful information
- To learn and remember main ideas and concepts
- To learn and remember main ideas, concepts, and selected details
- To analyze the book
- To evaluate the book
- To edit or proofread the book
- To memorize the book word-for-word

 Exercise 1: Determine Your Purpose (2 minutes)

1. Select one of your textbooks.

2. Think about what you want to get from the textbook, then reread the above list. Check the objectives that match your goal or make up your own specific purpose(s).

3. Write your purpose(s) here:

_____

_____

_____

_____

4. Are you prepared to stop reading when you've satisfied your purpose, but not before? If your answer is "yes," then your purpose is set. Otherwise, you need to reconsider. Pausing to set your purpose each time you start to read is a good habit to get into.

B. SURVEY READING

Once you've decided why you're reading a particular book, chapter, or article, you need to make a map to guide your steps in reading it. First, take a look at the material your reading will cover.

1. Surveying Textbooks

No matter what your purpose, getting "the big picture" or the main idea of what you'll be reading is worth your time. It can be done very quickly by doing a survey, and with a little practice, you can learn to survey an entire textbook in about five minutes or less. Try the following exercise using the textbook you used in the previous exercise. Read each step, then do it before moving on.

 Exercise 2: Survey Your Textbook (10 minutes)

1. Note the title of the book, the name of the author, and the date and place of publication. Is the book recently written? Is it out of date? Have you heard of the author before?

2. Think about what the title of the book means to you. What do you already know about the subject? Suppose your text is called *Child Psychology*. If you're a parent who is raising children, you probably have a good idea of the sort of information the book may contain. What questions come to mind? Jot down two or three questions. Then, guess what the chapter titles may be before going on.

3. Study the Contents page. Note the section and chapter headings. Did you correctly guess any chapter titles? Do you see any chapters or sections that will be especially useful to you?

   Why do you think it's organized this way? For example, a history book is usually laid out chronologically, showing a sequence of events over time. A biology book may start with discussions of the cell and move from there to larger units of living matter — first, the simplest plants and animals; then, the flowering plants and higher animals; then, humans. Why is your book organized the way it is?

4. Is there a reference list or bibliography? Are the references recent? Does the book have a glossary? An author index? A subject index? Answer these questions before moving on.

5. Where does the book begin? Where does it end? What is included and excluded?

6. Now try to remember the title and major headings. How many times have you described a good book to some friends, but then couldn't tell them its title or author? It takes practice and more than one quick survey to remember this information, so don't give up. Make remembering those headings the purpose of your survey.

You should only need to survey a textbook once or twice to get a clear picture of its contents. And your time will not be wasted as a thorough survey of a text actually decreases total reading time — in the same way that reading a map before a trip can save time.

2. Surveying Chapters

Before you read a particular chapter of a textbook, set your purpose and then survey the chapter. Surveying a chapter is generally more detailed than surveying an entire text, but it's a lot quicker. With some practice, you'll be able to do it in only two or three minutes.

Exercise 3: Surveying a Textbook Chapter
(10 minutes)

Pause and do each of the following steps before moving on.

1. Select a chapter from the same textbook you used earlier. Note the chapter title. What does it tell you about the content of the chapter? For example, in a biology textbook, what would a chapter called "Muscles and the Skeleton" tell you? It would probably be a description of parts of the skeleton and the different muscles and their interrelationships. What do you already know about your chapter? Take a minute to reflect and activate your prior knowledge.

2. Look at pictures, charts, graphs, diagrams, maps, etc. Read the captions for these illustrations and see if you can understand what they mean. How do these relate to the chapter title?

3. Read the headings and subheadings and note the overall organization of the chapter. Ask yourself if it makes sense. Can you tell why the author arranged the material in this way? How do the headings and subheadings relate to the chapter title?

4. Now, try to remember the major parts of the chapter. Again, don't give up after just one try. Good memory is based on actively thinking about the material several times.

5. Are there any questions or exercises in the chapter? Does the chapter have a short summary? These may be useful as a reading guide.

C. PREREADING: GETTING THE "GIST" OF THE CHAPTER

Now that you've done your survey and begun to establish a mental map to keep from losing your way, take a closer look at how the chapter has been structured to guide readers. Use this structure to take a closer look at the text.

 Exercise 4: Prereading a Textbook Chapter
(10 minutes)

1. Read the first paragraph (or the section headed "Introduction"). This is where the author should tell you what the chapter is all about.

2. If the chapter has a summary, read it now to overview the main points. If not, quickly read only the first sentence of each paragraph. In a well-organized text, this is usually also the topic sentence, telling you the content of that paragraph. If it doesn't, try the last sentence. But then go on to the next paragraph.

3. Now, take a moment to think about the important points. See if you can recall and recite the main ideas of the chapter. You may want to jot down a few of these points as a guide for note taking later.

You can practice this technique on your daily newspaper. In fact, probably the first thing you do when you pick it up is scan the major headlines and glance at any pictures, which is a form of surveying and prereading. After surveying your paper, see if you can recall the headlines. Use this survey to determine which stories you want to read in more detail.

By surveying and prereading a well-organized textbook chapter, you might obtain as much as 70% of the important information contained in it. In other words, you've learned the gist. So "prereading" means reading the first paragraph completely, and then reading the summary or the topic sentences in the rest of the chapter. You will now have a structured overview of the material in the chapter.

Sometimes, depending on your purpose, surveying and prereading a chapter may be all you need to do. If so, then stop reading. Usually, however, the survey and prereading are not enough. But now that you know where you're headed and what you'll encounter along the way, you can read more effectively.

II. FOCUS AND PERSPECTIVE FOR IMPROVING COMPREHENSION

No matter how well prepared you are for your textbook reading, it can sometimes be hard to locate the main idea, as it is often hidden by new vocabulary or disguised by an unfamiliar writing style. You'll find it easier to spot the theme if you practice often and try some of the approaches described here on material you're familiar with (like the newspaper).

A. DETERMINING THE FOCUS AND PERSPECTIVE

One thing you can do is locate the focus and perspective of the paragraph, sentence, or chapter. Suppose you have a camera and you decide to take a picture of your friend Jennifer. The person you want to focus on is Jennifer. Now you have to decide the angle of the picture. Will you take a profile, a head-to-toe, or an action shot? This angle is called the perspective. So when you take the picture of Jennifer, focus on her, but from a particular angle or perspective.

Now suppose that instead of photographing Jennifer, you want to verbally describe her. Jennifer is still the focus. That is, you're not talking about Michael or Stephanie or politics. You're talking about Jennifer. But Jennifer can be described in terms of her intellectual ability, her personality, her appearance, her job skills, and so on. The terms you use to describe her determine your perspective, just as the angle did with the camera.

Let's go one step further. What if you were reading a textbook entitled *Abnormal Psychology*? Using the title alone, what's the focus? What's the perspective?

"Psychology" is the focus; that is, the text will deal with psychology. But which aspect of psychology? Here the perspective is "abnormal."

Knowing the focus and perspective can really help reading comprehension. Read the following paragraph and try to determine what it is describing.

> *The procedure is actually quite simple. First you arrange things into different groups. Of course, one pile may be sufficient depending on how much there is to do. If you have to go somewhere else due to the lack of facilities that is the next step, otherwise you are pretty well set. It is important not to overdo things. That is, it is better to do too few things at once than too many. In the short run, this may not seem important but complications can easily arise. A mistake can be expensive as well. At first the whole procedure will seem complicated. Soon, however, it will become just another facet of life. It is difficult to foresee any end to the necessity for this task in the immediate future, but then one can never tell. After the procedure is completed, one arranges the materials into different groups again. Then they can be put into their appropriate places. Eventually they will be used once more, and the whole cycle will then have to be repeated. However, this is part of life.*

Does it have much meaning for you? Probably not. Could you recall the procedure on an exam? Again, probably not. There seems to be something missing — something fundamental. What's missing is a focus and perspective. Does it make more sense when you know that this paragraph is about washing clothes? The focus is now "clothes" and the perspective is "washing," not buying, making, or designing. Reread the paragraph with the focus and perspective in mind and see if it doesn't make complete sense. Try it now before moving on to Exercise 5.

 Exercise 5: Focus and Perspective (15 minutes)

As you go through the following examples, you'll find you are asked to give an answer before you continue. The "correct" answer will be located in the next box. If you get an answer wrong, try to understand why before going to the next question. Even though your answer may be different, you'll see whether you've understood the concept. These exercises will help you learn to locate the focus and perspective in sentences, paragraphs, or chapters, as well as in whole subject areas.

---

1. The following sentence is the introductory sentence of the first paragraph of a chapter in a biology textbook.

"The cattle tick is a small, flat-bodied, blood-sucking arachnid with a curious life history."

Focus: _____

Perspective: _____

Answer: Focus —*cattle tick*; Perspective —*life cycle*

2. Sometimes the focus and/or the perspective are not stated directly but are implied. For example, look at the following sentence.

   "The tundra is a vast treeless zone bordering the Arctic Ocean in North America, Europe and Asia."

   Focus: _____

   Perspective: _____

Answer: Focus — *the tundra*; Perspective — this is not stated directly, but it might be summarized as *description* or *characteristic* or *definition* or *geography*.

3. Now try a paragraph. This paragraph has only two sentences. First, see if you can find the topic sentence. This is the sentence that is most likely to contain the focus and perspective and that should introduce the central idea of the paragraph.

   For purposes of study, we can divide microeconomics into three main parts: the theory of demand, the theory of supply, and the theory of distribution. Each of these areas consists of a body of economic theory developed over the years and still under constant review.

   Mark the topic sentence.

Answer: *"For purposes of study, we can divide microeconomics into three main parts: the theory of demand, the theory of supply, and the theory of distribution."*

4. Now, in the sentence above, find the focus and perspective.

   Focus: _____

   Perspective: _____

Answer: Focus —*microeconomics*; Perspective —*three main parts (divisions).* So the important ideas we want to learn from that paragraph are the three main parts of microeconomics.

5. Now try a more difficult paragraph. Although the topic sentence is usually the first sentence, it isn't always. First, locate the topic sentence; then, locate the focus and perspective.

   Over the years, but particularly in the last two centuries, much has been thought and written about economic problems. Although controversy has surrrounded and continues to surround much of the discussion, we have come to understand much better the working of our economic system. Because of the breadth and complexity of the subject matter, it has become customary in recent years to divide economics into two main areas. Macroeconomics is the analysis of the behavior of the broad economic aggregates in society, such as national income, employment, inflation, and international trade; microeconomics is the analysis of the economic behavior of the various component elements of society, such as consumers, business firms, and resource owners, both as individuals and as groups.

Answer: Topic sentence — *"Because of the breadth and complexity of the subject matter, it has become customary in recent years to divide economics into two main areas."*

Focus — *economics*; Perspective — *the two main areas (divisions)*

Note the similarity to the focus and perspective of the previous paragraph.

B. Applying the Focus-and-Perspective Technique to Your Reading

There are four ways to relate the focus-and-perspective technique to your required reading.

1. When you have trouble concentrating, ask yourself if you can determine the focus and perspective of what you've just read. The process of trying to locate these factors forces you to concentrate and increases your understanding.

2. Finding the focus and perspective helps you determine the important points to learn. For instance, "divisions of microeconomics" lets you know that you should be able to answer the question "What are the divisions of microeconomics?".

3. If you can't find the focus and perspective, it may be because it is a poorly written paragragh or a chapter of little importance. Have you ever read something that didn't seem to contain any relevant information? In fact, the author may not have known the focus and perspective. Or, quite often, things are written with a focus but no perspective, and the reader is left with no idea of what was discussed, as in the paragraph on "washing clothes." So don't be in a hurry to blame yourself when you can't understand a paragraph or chapter. The writer may be at fault.

4. When taking and making notes, the focus and perspective give you a clue about what's important to record. This will be discussed in more detail in the section on taking and making notes from texts.

C. OTHER THINGS TO KEEP IN MIND WHEN LOOKING FOR FOCUS AND PERSPECTIVE

When reading, look for the points that the author considers important. In other words, note anything that is in **boldface** type or <u>underlined</u> (or emphasized) in any way.

Don't get mired in details; many are there only as examples or as illustrations of a point. The only important details are those that are necessary for understanding the topic.

Let words and punctuation help you. For instance, if you see a "however," "nevertheless," or "but," take note of what follows. Look at the following sentence: "Reading carefully is important, but don't let yourself get bogged down in details." The last part of the sentence is more important than the first, and the word "but" signals that importance.

Paragraphs are used for a reason, and a well-written paragraph should contain one main idea. So don't struggle to get too much from a paragraph. If you can find the focus and perspective, you'll have an essential clue to the important points.

III. INPUT AND OUTPUT

Many students see the primary goal of studying a textbook as "getting the information into their head." Although input is obviously necessary for learning, the "output" side of the process is perhaps more important for learning and remembering. For example, watching an accomplished painter apply splashes of color to a bare canvas or reading a how-to-paint book may help you learn to paint (input), but you'll need to practice painting in order to master it (output).

A. Asking Questions

One effective way to facilitate relevant input and output is to make up questions as you read. Once you have surveyed, preread, and determined the focus and perspective of a chapter, it's usually easy to ask yourself questions about the topic. Many students find that changing each heading into a question or two is enough to sharpen their input and to promote output. Almost any type of question will work: who, what, when, where, why, how, significance, etc.

Keep the question in mind as you read a section of the text. Look for the answers, and when you find them, recite (output) them.

B. Recitation

Recitation involves paraphrasing the main points in your own words without looking at the text. According to several studies, the time and effort involved in doing this are well worth it. Mental reciting is enough for some learners, but reciting aloud is usually even better. Better yet, recite to a classmate or friend.

 ## Exercise 6: Questioning and Reciting
(5 minutes)

1. Select a section of a textbook chapter containing some relevant information that is worth learning and remembering.

2. Change the heading into one or two questions.

3. Read the section for answers, reciting important points as you go.

4. When you can answer a question without looking at the text, then you've learned it and will likely remember it.

This technique of asking relevant questions, reading to find answers, and reciting the answers until they are learned can increase comprehension and memory several times.

IV. TAKING AND MAKING NOTES

No matter how carefully you read, you can't absorb or remember everything from a single reading. Surveying, prereading, and finding main ideas are important first steps. Another step involves taking and making notes.

Students usually take too many notes from their texts. Record only the important points. Otherwise, when you review your notes, it will be just like rereading the text. A good rule is: Never record or underline anything until you've finished reading the entire thought. Often, we write things down only to discover that they're covered more clearly later in the text, or that the thought wasn't that important at all.

Another good rule is: Underline or record something only if you can say it "from memory." If you can paraphrase something (and it's important), then it's okay to make a note. Copying or underlining something you don't understand is of little value.

Steps in Taking and Making Notes

- Always survey and preread your chapter before making notes of any kind.

- Make a chapter outline based on your survey and prereading. Leave space in the outline to add more details later (samples follow).

- Check your outline to see where you need more information. You may find that you noted most of the main ideas in your prereading. If so, when you return to read the chapter, just read what you think you need to.

- Read the chapter. Make a note of main ideas, vocabulary, and questions that come up as you go along. Underline important points or jot down comments or questions in the margin. Be careful not to underline too much.

For example, here's the paragraph we looked at earlier after an enthusiastic underliner got hold of it.

> For purposes of study, we can divide microeconomics into three main parts: the theory of demand, the theory of supply, and the theory of distribution. *Each of these areas consists of a body of economic theory developed over the years and still under constant review.*

Actually, the only information needed from this paragraph is that there are three main parts to microeconomic theory: demand, supply, and distribution.

- Finally, from your reading, add any additional basic ideas to the outline that you made after prereading.

V. ORGANIZING INFORMATION

A. WHY ORGANIZE?

Not only are we all familiar with the concept of organization, we use it daily. For example, imagine going grocery shopping with the following list:

hamburger	chicken
potatoes	pepper
apples	canned tomatoes
broccoli	carrots
raisins	celery
sugar	applesauce
flour	lentils
kidney beans	fish

The items are listed in that order because you jotted them down as you noticed what you needed that week. But would you buy things in that order? Probably not or you'd be running all over the store. You'd probably group together the items that are found in the same section of the store.

Exercise 7: Organize a Grocery List into Categories (4 minutes)

Group the 16 grocery items into four categories. What categories? Part of the benefit of organizing is the thinking involved in analyzing or synthesizing the information. To develop a categorization scheme, you must examine the information, look for common attributes, think of possible categories, and name or label the groups. These activities result in meaningful learning and improve remembering. As a warmup, try doing this with the 16 grocery items. In Exercise 8, we'll try it with a regular text chapter.

A:	B:	C:	D:

Can you organize the same items in a second way?

Exercise 8: Organize Ideas from a Text Chapter
(15 minutes)

Take a sheet of paper and cut or tear it into 16 pieces. Open your textbook to a chapter you haven't studied yet.

1. Survey the chapter using the method you learned on page 40.

2. During or after your survey, jot down key words or phrases onto the separate slips of paper — but only the key words or phrases. Go ahead.

3. Now close your text, shuffle the slips, and categorize them.

4. Next, preread the chapter using the method you learned on page 41. How was your preliminary organization? Does it need revision? Does your organization match the author's? Is your organization better?

Organizing information helps you in three main ways:

- It helps you keep track of things, saving time and effort as in the shopping list example.

- The process of analyzing and then rearranging items into categories helps you understand and remember material better.

- Organizing something also helps you see where you're missing information. What if you remembered you needed four items from the produce section, but had only picked up three? You'd then try very hard to remember that fourth item.

B. Kinds of Organization

Here's a list of Canadian place names. Could you remember it? Probably not for any length of time without repeating it again and again. How would you organize this list to be more meaningful for you? Try to do it before going on.

British Columbia	Ottawa	Regina
Ontario	Winnipeg	Lytton
University of British Columbia	Saskatoon	Royal Canadian Mint
	University of Manitoba	Victoria
University of Victoria	The Parliament Buildings	Saskatchewan
Hotel Vancouver	Vancouver	

1. Categorizing Information

One important way to organize pieces of information is to sort them into categories. You might have organized the place name items something like this:

Provinces	Cities	Universities	Buildings
British Columbia	Ottawa	University of British Columbia	Hotel Vancouver
Ontario	Winnipeg	University of Victoria	The Parliament Buildings
Saskatchewan	Saskatoon	University of Manitoba	Royal Canadian Mint
	Regina		
	Lytton		
	Victoria		
	Vancouver		

2. The Standard Outline

Now that you've sorted out the kind of information you have on the list, you can go one step further by demonstrating the relationship among the items in the different columns. When organizing information this way, you'd usually start with the largest or most important units and then show how the other items fit together. In our example, you could begin with the provinces and then show which cities are listed. Next, you would show the smaller items under the appropriate city. For British Columbia, the organization would be as follows:

British Columbia
   Victoria
      University of Victoria

   Vancouver
      University of British Columbia
      Hotel Vancouver

   Lytton

Note that the smaller items are indented to show the size or importance of the units. Items of equal importance are in line with each other (like Victoria, Vancouver and Lytton).

Exercise 9: Organizing Information to Show Relationships (5 minutes)

Now, try to arrange the rest of the list on a sheet of paper, following the pattern for British Columbia. If something is missing, leave a blank, but try to keep things indented correctly.

You've just worked through the method known as the standard outline, something you may have done in high school when writing essays. In that case, you may have used a system of numbers and letters (in addition to indenting) to show more clearly the levels of your organization. Applying that system to your list of place names, your outline would look like this:

Main Idea   I.   British Columbia
  Subheading   A.   Victoria
   Detail   1.   University of Victoria
           B.   Vancouver
               1.   University of British Columbia
               2.   Hotel Vancouver
           C.   Lytton

       II.   Saskatchewan
           A.   Saskatoon
           B.   Regina

      III.   Manitoba
           A.   Winnipeg
               1.   University of Manitoba

      IV.   Ontario
           A.   Ottawa
               1.   The Parliament Buildings
               2.   Royal Canadian Mint

Now that you've organized this information in two ways, ask yourself again, Can I remember that list? To test yourself, see if you can remember what appeared under British Columbia. What provinces were included, and what was listed under them? If you've done this exercise, chances are good you can now remember most of that 16-item list.

 Exercise 10: Making a Standard Outline
(10 minutes)

Here's part of a chapter from an economics textbook. See if you can take notes from this, fitting them into the outline that follows it.

Economics

Over the years, but particularly in the last two centuries, much has been thought and written about the economic problem. Although controversy has surrounded and continues to surround much of the discussion, we have come to understand much better the working of our economic system. Because of the breadth and complexity of the subject matter, it has become customary in recent years to divide economics into two main areas. Macroeconomics is the analysis of the behavior of the broad economic aggregates in society, such as national income, employment, inflation, and international trade; microeconomics is the analysis of the economic behavior of the various elements of society, such as consumers, business firms, and resource owners, both as individuals and as groups.

Microeconomics

For the purposes of study, we can divide microeconomics into three main parts: the theory of demand, the theory of supply, and the theory of distribution. Each of these areas consists of a body of economic theory developed over the years and still under constant review.

The theory of demand attempts to explain why individuals, business firms, and governments buy goods and services; how their spending pattern is determined; and the nature of the relationship between demand on the one hand and marketplace and income on the other. In this attempt, the theory of demand makes use of such concepts as total and marginal utility, indifference curves and budget lines, demand schedules and demand curves, and price-and-income elasticities of demand.

Economics

2 branches of economics	I. _____
	II. _____
3 divisions of 1 branch	A. _____
	B. _____
	C. _____

Your outline will probably look something like this:

Economics

I. **Macroeconomics**
II. **Microeconomics**
    A. **Theory of demand**
    B. **Theory of supply**
    C. **Theory of distribution**

When you developed your outline, did you use some of the suggestions made earlier in this section?

Did you:

- look at the heading and think about it?

- analyze the word "microeconomics" to guess what it might mean? (micro means "small")

- look for the topic sentence in the general discussion about economics?

- note that the second paragraph begins with the topic sentence?

Try this method of note taking using your regular text. It isn't easy at first, but doing it will increase comprehension and facilitate memory.

3. Tables for Organizing Information

Look at the list of Canadian place names again. You could turn it into a table, grouping the names as follows:

Provinces	Cities	Universities	Buildings
British Columbia	Victoria	University of Victoria	
	Vancouver	University of British Columbia	
			Hotel Vancouver
	Lytton		
Saskatchewan	Regina		
	Saskatoon		
Ontario	Ottawa		

Suppose you had a history chapter to learn. You could set up your table by country, like this:

BY COUNTRY

THEMES IN HISTORY	Persia	Rome	Egypt
Economic			
Cultural			
Political			
Scientific			
Colonization			

Begin by surveying and then prereading the chapter to note the kinds of information about the three different countries. From that initial work, develop a grid pattern similar to the one shown here. When you return to read the chapter in detail, put the information in the boxes. Of course, at times you might find you didn't leave enough space, or the headings you picked don't quite fit and need to be revised. Don't look on this as a failure or as wasted time. What you're doing is thinking about your studies, working with the ideas, and sorting them out. In fact, if you had to rework your organization of the data in the text, it's that part you'll likely remember best.

Here's another example, this time from a geography textbook. You might be studying a chapter on biomes, the different areas of climate and location in the world. In that case, you may find, after surveying and prereading the chapter, that each section basically provides four types of information for each biome. Your organization would look like this.

BIOMES	Average Temp	Average Rainfall	Plant Life	Animal Life
Prairies				
Northern Forests				
Tropical Forests				
Deserts				

By looking at the grid, are you already beginning to get a good idea of what a biome is? An organizational pattern not only helps you remember, it's also a useful tool for helping you understand and extract the important parts of a text.

 ## Exercise 11: Organizing with Tables
(20 minutes)

Using a text chapter you've already surveyed and preread (perhaps the one you used in the previous exercise), construct a table to represent information in the text. You may be able to just skim the chapter to fill in the grid.

---

4. Flow Diagrams for Organizing Information

Not all textbook material lends itself to organization in grid form. Sometimes information shows a course of development, a sequence of events, a procedure, or the like. In such cases, a flow diagram is a good way to represent the information when you're taking notes from the text. A good example is the life cycle. It can be represented like this:

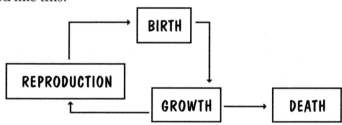

(After reproduction, a new organism is born while the original one eventually dies.)

The arrow in a flow diagram can mean several things:

- a step in procedure; a sequence of events (growth follows birth)
- "causes" (reproduction causes birth)
- "leads to" (growth eventually leads to death)

Here is a paragraph from a text. See if you can make a flow diagram for it.

All verbal information goes first into the primary memory (short-term memory). When it is rehearsed (recited), part of it goes into our secondary (long-term) memory. The rest of it, usually the part we are least interested in, is forgotten.

Here is one way you could diagram this,

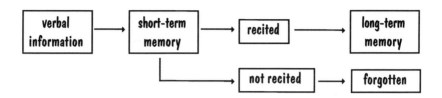

This short paragraph is also a reminder of how important it is to recite material in order to remember it (see Section 3, page 49). A one-time reading of a paragraph or chapter simply is not enough to fully understand and remember complex information. You need some kind of back-up system — an oral or written reminder of what it was you discovered when reading.

 Exercise 12: Organizing by Flow Chart
(10 minutes)

The next time you come across reading or lecture material that describes a procedure or a cause-effect relationship or a sequence of related events, try making a simple flow chart to organize and summarize the information.

5. Doodling to Represent Information

Doodling is an informal way to take notes. You've likely sat in a lecture or meeting and doodled while the speaker went on and on. Sometimes your doodling began to reflect some of the speaker's words. These little scribbles you make as you try to understand ideas can actually be channelled into constructive ways of learning. Anyone can doodle, and the process can help immensely with both understanding and learning. Consider the following example of a doodle representing a student's understanding of Shakespeare's play *Romeo and Juliet*.

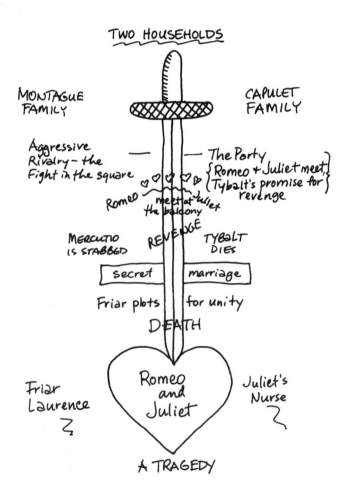

Exercise 13: Doodling to Organize Information

Try doodling the following description of the tundra.

The tundra is a vast treeless zone bordering the Arctic Ocean in North America, Europe, and Asia. It generally extends from the treeline to the areas perpetually covered with ice and snow. Obviously, this area has a cold climate: the ground remains permanently frozen to within a few inches of the surface, and the growing season is only about 60 days. There is also an alpine tundra on the peaks and high slopes of mountains, as in the western Rocky Mountains, the Alps, and the Himalayan Mountains.

In general, tundra vegetation consists of lichens, mosses, grasses, and dwarfed woody plants. The composition of the vegetation in any particular portion of the tundra varies with the thickness and fertility of the soil. Grasses and sedges compose the alpine tundra. In all cases, numerous adaptations for survival in this extreme environment are found: dwarfism, small hairy leaves for water conservation, ability to survive in the frozen state even when flowering, and means of vegetative reproduction. We might suppose that animal life would be sparse under these conditions, but this is not true throughout the year. During the summer great numbers of waterfowl nest in the tundra, and several species of insects — especially mosquitoes and black flies — are abundant. Permanent residents are few. Small rodents, including the well-known lemmings, are the most abundant mammals. Other characteristic forms of animal life are caribou (reindeer in Eurasia), Arctic hare, Arctic fox, gray wolf, grizzly bear, polar bear, and the snowy owl. These forms show adaptation for winter survival, including white coloration, ability to hibernate for periods of time, and means for burrowing under the snow.

This one is up to your imagination. The sky's the limit when doodling.

6. Hierarchies for Organizing Information

While you're in the mood to do some drawing, here's another way to pull information from a text. Sometimes material in a chapter is organized in various levels or hierarchies. Hierarchies are also something we encounter every day — most of us work in a type of hierarchy, with people working both above and below us.

Remember the list of place names? The names could be arranged in a hierarchy as follows:

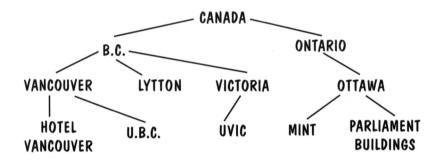

You could also reorganize the notes on microeconomics in a hierarchy.

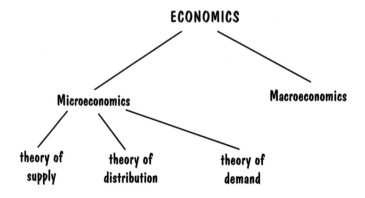

Exercise 14: Make a Hierarchy to Organize Information

Make a hierarchy for the following passage from a history text.

> *In the fifteenth and sixteenth centuries, Europe embarks on the conquest of the rest of the world . . . the social structure at this time in Europe resembles a pyramid. The top of the pyramid represents the person or persons who hold political power. The king is the supreme authority, the sovereign. Moreover, he tries to make the people believe that his authority comes from God. Under his domination are the nobles, who are really little kings, each in his own province. The nobles in turn dominate the masses, the peasants, who work their seigneur's land in return for little more than bare subsistence. The peasants live in a kind of slavery. The seigneur is master with nearly absolute authority over them.*

VI. INCREASING READING SPEED

How fast do you read now? Get a friend to time you while you read some fairly easy material for one minute, and then count the number of words you read. You now know how many words per minute (wpm) you read. If you read less than 250 wpm, some of the following tips might help.

A. SPEED TIPS

- Preread and survey first. You'll find your reading speed will increase once you know what to expect in your reading.

- Try looking at small groups of words rather than one word at a time. If you move your lips while you read, you're likely reading only one word at a time. To help break this habit, try pointing with your finger two or three times per line and following your finger with your eyes. This takes practice!

- Not every word in a book is worth reading. Some words are more important than others. Think about putting a classified ad in the newspaper. You omit all but the absolutely essential words to say the maximum amount at the lowest price. Treat reading the same way: read only the essential words and skim the others. For instance, this paragraph could be read like this:

  **Not every word worth reading/Some more important/
  Read necessary words/Skim others/**

- Read more. The more you read, the more confident you'll be of your reading ability.

- Take a few minutes each day to practice reading at a faster-than-comfortable speed. If you normally read three pages in two minutes, try to get through six pages. Then, see if you can summarize what you've read. This will help increase your normal reading rate.

B. MEASURING PROGRESS

If you want to increase your reading speed, use the speed tips and measure your reading speed once in a while. Use this graph to plot your speed each time you measure your reading rate. (Be sure to read material with the same level of difficulty each time.) It's quite easy to increase your reading speed, but it does take practice.

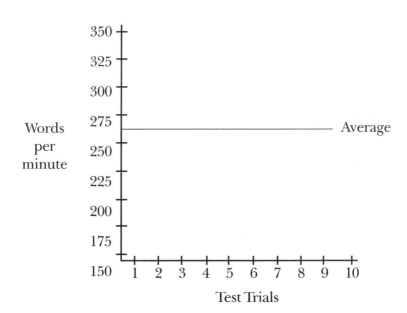

VII. SUMMARY

There are several ways to take notes from your textbooks, and all of them will help you understand and remember the material. But some of these methods will work better than others, depending on the type of material you're reading. If you're a visual person, you may like the ideas of doodling, flow diagrams, and hierarchies. If you're more print-oriented, try the tables or standard outline. There is certainly more to it than running your eyes over the line of print. Start in and work with the material. You may find that it makes reading and studying a lot more enjoyable and certainly more productive.

Here is a summary outline of the reading methods described in this section. We are confident that the selective use of these methods will, with practice, improve your reading efficiency and strengthen your comprehension and memory. Try out the techniques on a chapter or two, experiment with different combinations, and evaluate your reading. Use the outline as a checklist when you read.

A. **Purpose** (2 minutes)
   1. Why are you reading it?
   2. How much detail should you learn?
      a. What should you know when you're finished?
      b. What questions could you ask?

B. **Survey and Prereading** (5 minutes)
   1. Survey chapter
      a. Title
      b. Figures, tables, illustrations, etc.
      c. Headings
   2. Preread chapter
      a. Introduction
      b. Summary
      c. First/last sentences in paragraphs
      d. Questions and exercises
   3. Focus and Perspective

C. Form Questions
1. What do you already know about the topic?
2. What questions do you want to answer as you read?
3. Change headings into questions

D. Recite
1. Paraphrase important information
2. Answer questions
3. Practice remembering

E. Organize
1. Categories
2. Outlines
3. Tables
4. Flow Charts
5. Doodles
6. Hierarchies

4

Writing Essays and Reports

Survey Your Present Writing Habits

		Always	Almost Always	Usually	Sometimes	Almost Never	Never
1	I write something (letter, paper, diary, etc.) every week.						
2	I enjoy writing.						
3	I find it easy to come up with ideas for a paper.						
4	My papers are well organized.						
5	Readers understand my main ideas						
6	I do an outline before I write.						
7	I research my papers.						
8	I ask myself questions to answer in my papers.						
9	I skim reference material first to see if it's relevant.						
10	I write a rough draft, then edit it to compose a paper.						
11	I reread and double-check the assignment on a regular basis.						
12	I begin a writing assignment the day it's given.						
13	I use the instructor's guidelines for form, style, and language.						
14	I proofread twice before handing in a paper.						

If you answered "always" or "almost always" to most of these survey items, you probably have little difficulty writing papers. Otherwise, read over the information and try the exercises.

I.   WRITING

Although you may not have any experience writing formal assignments, you do have writing experience: letters, high school essays, business forecasts, volunteer work, even poems and stories you've done. But, in spite of this experience, you may not be very confident about your writing ability and find the idea of written assignments less than appealing.

You may also wonder why writing papers is necessary. Writing is a part of everyday life, and the skills you develop to do written assignments will always be of use to you. Assigned essays and reports give you the opportunity to learn and practice research, organizational, and logical-thought skills. Writing assignments also help you develop your knowledge of a particular subject or a field of study. You learn most when you dig out information yourself and then try to organize it so that someone else can understand your written description of what you've found.

Writing is definitely hard work. But once you learn a few of the basic steps, you may find that working on reports helps you learn what you need or want to know.

II. DECIDING WHAT TO WRITE

If you have a choice of topic, the following guidelines will help you choose the best one for you.

A. GIVING YOURSELF TIME TO SELECT A TOPIC

Even if you have writing experience, it still takes time to come up with ideas. The best approach is to start thinking about possible topics and writing down ideas as soon as you know you have a paper to prepare.

B. PICKING SOMETHING OF INTEREST TO YOU

For example, if you have been asked to make a comparison and you are interested in buying a car, do a comparison of the advantages and disadvantages of leasing versus buying. If you are to write a history paper on a topic of your choice, pick an event or time from history that you find fascinating.

C. LIMITING YOUR TOPIC TO THE PRESCRIBED LENGTH AND TIME

For instance, if you want to write about urban transit and your report is supposed to be between 700 and 1,000 words, you'll have to pick a particular aspect of it, or your paper may be too long. To narrow down a topic, you become increasingly specific, as follows:

Urban transit
Urban transit in Canada
Urban transit in British Columbia
LRT service in British Columbia
LRT service on Vancouver Island

You can try these steps no matter what your interests are.

Exercise 1: Narrowing a Topic by Making It More Specific (5 minutes)

Select one of these topics, then progressively narrow it by making each subtopic more specific.

> The advantages of teaching music to children
> Italian cooking
> The environment
> Trends in health care
> Municipal politics

D. PICKING A TOPIC YOU KNOW WELL OR WANT TO KNOW BETTER

If you're trying to improve your writing style, work with something familiar. When you're not sure what you're talking about, it's hard to put together a clear and organized essay that someone else can understand.

III. WHAT IT TAKES TO WRITE A REPORT

For a report or term paper, you need to gather information from books, professional journals, computer sources, direct observations, or interviews, and then present that information in an organized fashion. In other words, you must research a topic and draw together information from a number of sources. Here are some guidelines to get you started.

A. BRAINSTORMING

Digging information out of various sources is usually the basis for your research. But it's easy to get buried in information if you don't have some idea of what you're looking for. To avoid that overload, begin by asking yourself questions about your topic — as many as you can. Don't worry about answers, or whether the questions are important or relevant. Just let your mind flow and ask who, what, where, why, how, and so what. This free-flowing process, known as brainstorming, will help you reduce your job to a manageable level.

Brainstorming has a number of benefits. Initially, it helps you decide "What do I want to know about this topic?" It then helps you cut down on research time because, instead of reading everything you find on the topic, you read and skim selectively to find answers to your questions. Brainstorming can also be the first step toward organizing your information. By writing your questions on small pieces of paper, you can shuffle the questions around to see which ones fit together, which ones would make a good beginning or ending, and which ones are not needed. As you do this, you may come up with a few more questions.

Depending on the topic, brainstorming may lead to many questions (20, 30, or more), not all of which you'll answer in your paper. Sometimes, though, it's hard to think up questions to ask. To get started, talk to someone about your topic or look it up in a general reference (like an encyclopedia). Knowing at least a little about the topic should make it easier for you to come up with some relevant questions. Here are some general brainstorming questions you could use:

1. What is it?
2. What does it mean?
3. How is it put together?
4. How does it work?
5. Why is it the way it is?
6. How did it come to be this way?
7. When did it occur or exist?
8. What is it worth?
9. What is its importance?
10. How well does it fulfill its intended function?
11. Who originated it?
12. Where is it used?

Exercise 2: Brainstorming Questions
(5 minutes)

You've been asked to write a paper on "Women in Politics." Write one question relating to this topic for each of the question words below.

Who: _____

What: _____

When: _____

Where: _____

Why: _____

How: _____

Here are some questions you might have asked.

Who are they?
Who was the first woman to enter Canadian politics?
What obstacles have there been in the past?
What background prompts women to run for office?
What personal qualities do some present female politicians have?
When did B.C. elect its first woman MP or MLA?
Where in Canada is there the greatest proportion of women politicians?
Why do women enter politics?
Why aren't there many female political figures in Canada?
Why is it important for women to be in politics?
How does the number of women in Canadian politics compare with the number in other countries?
How does a woman get started in politics? Is it different from a man's start?
How have women in politics influenced legislation?
How does a career in politics affect women's lives and families?

Exercise 3: Brainstorming Ideas for a Paper

Do this exercise with an actual writing assignment. If you don't have an assignment, but want to practice, pick a topic and follow these steps.

1. Make up about 30 small slips of blank paper or use index cards.

2. On 5 cards, write "Who." Then continue and write 5 cards each with "What," "When," "Where," "Why," and "How."

3. Now, starting with a "Who" card, develop a question that explores some aspects of the topic you've chosen.

4. Does that question lead to others? Write them down and try to fill all 30 cards with one question each. Go ahead.

   If you get stuck, change your perspective — this time change your "time" perspective. For example, ask questions that someone may want answered 100 years from now. The goal is to come up with as many questions as possible so you can then select a few of the ideas to research and explore.

5. Save all your questions cards for Exercise 4. But before going to it, read the next section.

B. ORGANIZING YOUR QUESTIONS INTO A GENERAL OUTLINE

Go over your question cards and decide which ones go together. Then, see if you can put these groups into a logical order. You may end up with groups that look something like this:

- Definition of terms and introduction
- Background information/history
- Significant figures
- Significant events
- Future predictions

If you've been assigned a topic, this is the time to make sure you know what is being asked. For instance, if you've been asked to describe something, you won't evaluate or critize it. (You'll find explanations of these terms at the end of this section.) Use your brainstorming and initial research to decide on a general organization or outline for your report.

After you've made your general outline, list the questions you want to answer under each heading. At this point, you may either want to omit some of your original questions or have found more questions to answer.

For example, to organize the questions on "Women in Politics," you may have first divided them into two categories: past and present. Now, using these main headings, you could group your questions as shown below.

Sample Outline for "Women in Politics"

I.   **First Women in Canadian Politics**

    A.   Who was the first woman to enter Canadian politics?

    B.   When did B.C. elect its first woman?

    C.   What significant contributions did these women make?

II. **Women in Politics Today**

    A.   Who are they?

    B.   How did they get started?

    C.   Why did they enter politics?

    D.   What personal qualities do they have?

    E.   Does it affect their lives and families?

Exercise 4: Organizing Your Questions
(15 minutes)

1. Arrange the 30 question cards from Exercise 3 into groups that tend to deal with the same issue or idea.

2. Do some questions go together naturally? Do some questions not fit at all? Move the cards around to try to come up with a grouping that suits the assignment. Note: It's a good idea to reread the assignment every so often to make sure you're on the right track.

3. Construct an outline using all the relevant questions and omitting those that don't belong.

4. Save your general outline for Exercise 5.

Are you remembering to take breaks?

C. NARROWING YOUR TOPIC

After completing the first two steps — brainstorming and initial organizing — you may find yourself with many questions that deal with one particular aspect of your topic. You may decide to limit your paper to a discussion of just this aspect.

For instance, there are many ways to narrow down the "Women in Politics" topic. Here's one way:

1. Women in Politics (general topic)

2. Women in Politics, 1975 to 1995 (narrowed down in time)

3. Women in Canadian Politics, 1975 to 1995 (politics narrowed down)

4. Significant Women in Canadian Politics, 1975 to 1995

As you can see, the last topic is much more specific than the first one and likely to be an easier topic to manage. You now have a concrete focus and perspective (see Section 3, page 42). The focus is Canadian politics; the perspective is significant women.

 Exercise 5: Narrowing Your Topic (15 minutes)

1. Look at the outline you constructed in Exercise 4. Can your topic be limited to part of your outline?

2. Once you've narrowed your topic, rewrite your outline, adding and deleting questions and making sure it has a clear focus and a clear perspective.

3. Read the assignment over again at this stage. Do you have enough questions, or too many? Would the answers to your questions be interesting? Make revisions as necessary.

You've now completed two of the most important steps in writing a well-organized paper: you've narrowed the topic and made an outline.

Many writers put their first outline aside for a day or two, so they can return to it fresh and make revisions. The time you've spent focusing your topic will be well worth it as you move to the next step — research.

IV. RESEARCH: LOCATING INFORMATION AND MODIFYING YOUR OUTLINE

Research consists of finding answers to the questions you've brainstormed. It may also lead to more brainstorming and to a revision of your outline. Look at your topic and choose some key words that you can use for locating information. For instance, for the topic "Significant Women in Canadian Politics," you could start by looking up "Canada — politics" in the library's information system. A recent book on Canadian politics might include some information about significant female politicians, which would give you a starting point for your research. Where exactly do you find this information? Here are some suggestions.

A. RESOURCES

- **Encyclopedias**. While not sufficient as references, they can often point to other places to check or to key words to use.

- **Your textbooks**. The reference list at the back of your textbooks may have the names of relevant articles or books.

- **The library**. Look up your topic on the various information systems available in the library for a list of books or articles available on your topic. These may range from card catalogue and periodical indexes to computerized on-line searches. Ask a librarian for help when using these if you're not familiar with them. They can be a little complicated to use, but will be very worthwhile if you're working on topics related to current issues.

- **Resource people in the community**. There may be a significant woman politician in your town, or perhaps someone who knows such a woman.

- **Friends and family**. Ask other people for help. Even someone not taking the same course may have some good suggestions.

Consider the time period you need to cover in your search. Would a book or article published five years ago be out of date?

B. RECORDING THE INFORMATION

Use a notebook to record information on books and articles that may be of use to you. Record not only the author's full name and the complete title, but also the place of publication, publisher, date of publication, and the page numbers in the case of a journal article, as well as the library call number. For example,

---

Dunung, Sanjyot P.
HF 3826.5
W676

Doing Business in Asia:
The Complete Guide
New York: Lexington Books, 1995

Silk, Joseph
QB 981
S56

A Short History of the Universe
New York: Scientific American Library,
1994

Although you may locate many titles (several pages worth), you'll actually find only some of the books or articles in the library. This is one very good reason to begin your research early.

As you search for each book or article you've listed, note the outcome of your search beside each title. That is, it is:

- out on loan

- out, but you reserved it

- found, but not suitable

- found and checked out

This will help you keep track of your references and save you time in the long run.

1. General Rules

Here are a few general rules for recording information that will improve your research skills and save time.

- Keep your basic outline beside you as you read to keep you on track.

- Do one reference at a time. Decide if it will be useful to you by examining the contents page and the index, and by skimming the preface and introductory chapter. Always skim first, and then read only the parts that relate directly to your topic and your questions.

- Use a separate sheet of paper to begin notes on each reference you use.

- Use only one side of each sheet to record information, and number the pages if you have more than one for a reference.

2. Getting the Information on Paper

- For each reference you decide to make notes on, write the complete reference citation (call number, author's full name, title, and details of publication) at the top of a sheet (see the sample Reference Sheet that follows). You'll need all this information to write your reference list or bibliography.

- As you read, write summary statements of the information you need, and then note the page(s) where you found it. If you quote directly from anything, use quotation marks. Leave a line or two between each summary. (For tips on making notes, see pages 50 to 51.)

Example: Reference Sheet

Dunung, Sanjyot P.   *Doing Business in Asia:*
HF 3826.5   *The Complete Guide*
W676   New York: Lexington Books, 1995

A comprehensive handbook for doing business in 20 Asian countries.
    p. 175 — few large companies in Taiwan; most are small, family owned, family controlled;

    p. 177 — business conducted in social setting in Taiwan; usually at dinner, sometimes at lunch, rarely at breakfast.

- When you've recorded all the relevant information from a book or article, clip your notes together and set them aside. Do this for each reference you use. As you do your research, expand and modify your outline.

- After you finish this part of your research, you should have several piles of notes. Each pile, clipped together, has the information from a single source and the bibliographic information(title, author, publisher, date, etc.). And in front of you, you'll have an expanded and modified outline.

V. ORGANIZING YOUR FINAL OUTLINE FOR WRITING

In Exercise 5, you narrowed your topic and made an outline based on your brainstorming questions. Now that you've researched and collected more information, you need to integrate this with the outline before you can start writing. Depending on the new information, you may also need to make a new and final outline.

Types of Outlines for Writing

Here are some ways to organize the content of a topic into an outline for writing.

A. CHRONOLOGICAL

When developments occur in a time sequence, your outline can be arranged in order of time.

B. COMPARATIVE

When your material involves comparisons, whether point by point, by theories, by states, by styles, etc., you can organize a comparative essay in one of two ways. For instance, if you were to compare private and public schools, it could be organized in either of these ways:

Method 1	*Method 2*
Private Schools vs. Public Schools	Private Schools vs. Public Schools

I.	Private Schools	I.	Teachers	
	A. Teachers		A.	Private Schools
	B. Classes		B.	Public Schools
	C. Activities	II.	Classes	
II.	Public Schools		A.	Private Schools
	A. Teachers		B.	Public Schools
	B. Classes	III.	Activities	
	C. Activities		A.	Private Schools
			B.	Public Schools

C. TOPICAL

The ideas are categorized by primary idea, secondary idea, etc., as in the example in Method 1 above.

D. PROBLEM — SOLUTION

For a paper concerned with problem solving, state the problem, then the various solutions.

E. OPINION — REASON

A statement of opinion is given, followed by reasons and evidence to support it. For example: "There are many advantages of teaching swimming to young children."

Your revised outline will probably look something like the standard outlines we talked about in the Reading and Remembering section of this handbook. Sometimes, going over your outline with the instructor or with friends is helpful — they may ask important questions that you missed. Once this final outline is done, stick to it when you write so you aren't sidetracked. It helps to put at least part of your outline in sentence form. These sentences can then become the topic (or first) sentences of paragraphs in your essay.

VI. ORGANIZING RESEARCH NOTES TO MATCH YOUR OUTLINE

So far you have:

- selected a general topic
- narrowed your topic
- made a general outline to guide your research
- researched your topic and made research notes
- revised your outline

The next step is to go through your research notes and decide where the information fits into your outline. That is, you need to shuffle and sort your research notes so the information matches the organization of your outline.

Two methods of coding research notes are explained on pages 94 and 95. But first, look over this sample outline.

Effects of Reaganomics

I.   Introduction
II. Background and Definitions
    A.   Definition of "Reaganomics"
    B.   Distinctions between Supply-side and Demand-side Theories
        1. Supply-side Theory
           a) Money Supply
           b) Consumer Spending
           c) Government Spending
        2. Demand-side Theory
           a) Money Supply
           b) Consumer Spending
           c) Government Spending

III. Short-term Effects of Supply-side Economics in the United States
    A.   Changes in Inflation
        1. Money Supply
        2. Consumer Spending
        3. Government Spending
    B.   Changes in Unemployment

IV. Long-term Effects of Supply-side Economics in the United States
    A.   Changes in Inflation
        1. Money Supply
        2. Consumer Spending
        3. Government Spending
    B.   Changes in Unemployment

V.   Conclusions

Method 1: Coding Your Research Notes to Your Outline

1. Read through your research notes, summary by summary. After reading a summary, look at the outline and decide if the note is relevant to any part of it. Some of your notes will not be relevant; others may fit into one or more places in the outline. For some parts of your outline, you may have no relevant notes and may need to do more research. For other parts, you may have several relevant summary notes.

    For example, in reading the research notes from one source, you might find a summary with information relating to the "Money Supply" aspect of "Supply-side Theory." When you look at your outline, you'll see that this summary fits into Section II.B.1.a).

    In the margin of that research note, you would write II.B.1.a) to indicate that the note will be used when you write that section of the paper.

    In the same way, a summary note relating to the "Effects of Supply-side Economics" on "Unemployment" might best fit into Section III.B. or Section IV.B., depending on whether it refers to short- or long-term effects.

2. As you read through your summary notes and code relevant summaries to your outline, you'll begin to see how the paper will flow from subtopic to subtopic. You may come across some useful information in your notes that won't fit in the outline, but should be included in the paper. If the information is really relevant to your topic, adjust your outline to include it, but don't get sidetracked by irrelevant information.

3. When you finish, you'll have your research notes coded to the outline. As you work on each section, refer to the summaries that are coded to that particular part.

Method 2: "Cut and Paste" Research Notes

1. After coding each relevant summary statement from your re-
    search notes (using Method 1), color code each reference sheet
    of your notes by drawing a line down the side of the sheet.

    Use a different color for each reference sheet you plan to use.
    Note that the color code runs the entire length of the sample
    sheet.

Example: Reference Sheet with Color Code

color code
(e.g., red stripe)

Brown, J.T. Unemployment and supply-side
economics. Economic Review, 1983, 4(3),
187-193.

III.B. Short-term unemployment under
Reaganomics increased 23% in areas of primary
industry. page 187

IV.B. Projected long-term unemployment was
expected to be greatest in areas dependent on
government contracts ... page 189

(not used) New York's women's unemployment
rates were virtually unaffected by economic
policies in contrast to other states.
page 189

IV.B. Some theorists (E.B. Teller, for example)
predicted that supply-side economics may ulti-
mately lead to a gradual reduction in U.S.
unemployment to post WWII levels. page 188

2. Cut off the summary statements so that each summary is on a separate slip of paper. Save the bibliographic information slip with its colored line — this is your key to coding.

3. Organize the slips of paper to match your outline. Tape them together.

4. Your research notes are now organized into a detailed outline that you can follow as you write your first draft. The colored lines through each piece of information tell you where you got the information.

5. Put the slips of bibliographic information that you used into alphabetical order. This becomes your reference list.

VII. FROM OUTLINE TO FINAL PRODUCT

Now that you've completed the organization of your research notes, you're ready to begin your first draft. Not only do you have extensive notes, you should know your topic well enough to express yourself fluently. If you don't feel this way, you may need to study your research, or even do more of it. You'll be ready to start writing when you know what you want to say and can express it clearly to both yourself and others.

As you prepare to write, consider your audience. Your instructor, of course, is your real audience, but it may help to imagine your fellow students as your audience. They'll be less intimidating because they're not likely to know much about your topic, and this makes you the resident expert in the field. And if your writing is aimed at them, it will force you to write more clearly and to explain things in more detail than you might otherwise. In other words, you'll write a better essay.

When you write a paper, take the general attitude that:

- your paper is targeted at someone who is virtually ignorant of the topic, and it is your job to explain everything that falls outside the realm of "common knowledge"

- you are trying to convince this person that your argument is valid

A. THE COMPLETED ESSAY

When you're ready to begin writing your first draft, it helps to have a mental picture of the final product.

Your completed essay will have six elements.

1. Title Page

A discussion of the title page and other formatting details (size of paper, typing/word-processing instructions, etc.) are found in the instructor's Style Sheet (ask your instructor).

2. Introduction

The first paragraph or two should give your reader a clear understanding of what your essay is about. The following list gives you an idea of what you need to include in your introduction.

- **Purpose for writing**: State your topic and how you present it.

  Example: "The purpose of this paper is to describe and analyze the main kinds of family systems that exist in the United States and Canada."

- **Lines of development**: State or list the subtopics you use in your essay (these may be from the list of categories in your outline).

  Example: "The analysis will focus on the range of 'relatives' included in a family system, the social organization of the family group, and the role relationships existing within the system."

- **Define terms**: You may need to define specialized terms or words with multiple meanings that you want to use in a specific sense. Make sure the reader knows exactly how such key words are used in your paper.

  Example: "The discussion is limited to families from the 'immigrant' peoples of North America and excludes family systems from the 'Native' peoples."

- **Present thesis**: A thesis statement could state your position on the topic. In this case, the reader assumes that your whole essay attempts to prove or disprove this position.

    Example: "This paper examines how the works of English Canadian writers Morley Callahan, Edward McCourt, and Sinclair Ross reflected important trends in society during this decade."

- **Provide background to topic**: You can take the opportunity to state your reason for writing about this topic or why the topic is important to write about.

3. Body

This is the substance of your essay, where you "talk" to your reader about the things you stated in your introduction.

It's a good idea to review your outline to decide the best way to present your topic. (See the upcoming section on "action words" for organizational ideas that match your presentation.)

As a general guideline, use the following steps to develop your main points.

- **Preface, then state your point simply and clearly.**

    Example: "Keeping with the subject of therapeutic pastimes, gardening is another very enjoyable vocation."

- **Develop the point beyond this brief statement.**

    Example: "Faced with the pressures of modern living, many people turn to working with plants to relax themselves and to gain a respite from their everyday lives. From a variety of sources, it appears that personal gardening is on the increase."

- **Support general statements with quotes and/or statistics.**

    Example: "Evidence of this is to be found in the rapid growth of organizations that serve gardeners. In the past two years, garden clubs and horticultural associations have reported significant numbers of new members. An estimate of gardeners actively affiliated with these organizations numbers in the two million range, according to Greg Green, president of the Canadian Horticultural Association."

- **Illustrate with examples.**

  Example: "One organization, the Canadian Flower Association, has recently purchased an estate for its new headquarters to serve a membership that has tripled in the past 18 months."

- **Conclude and interrelate with your other main points.**

  Example: "In addition to general associations, many more specialized groups, such as the B.C. Rhododendron Society, have been spawned by the general boom. However, such has not been the fate of the once popular pastime of model railroading."

4. Transitions

Of all the mechanical aspects of a paper (aside from basic grammar and spelling), transitions are essential to the success of your essay. Basically, transitions:

- help the reader move smoothly from one point to the next

- remind the reader how each section of your essay relates to your overall theme and purpose

Smoothness is achieved by using transition words and phrases where they're appropriate — that is, use "first," "second," "next," "in addition to," "finally," "consequently," "as a result," "however," "therefore," etc.

A simple statement of how a particular point fits into your argument will fulfill the second purpose of transitions. Use this technique if you think there is any chance the reader may be confused without such a statement.

5. Conclusion

Don't stop after the last item in your argument — always have some kind of concluding statement.

You may choose to do some or all of these things in your conclusion:

- summarize or review the content and thesis of your essay

- discuss questions for further research. If you were to write a sequel to your essay, what would the logical topic be?

- discuss implications and/or applications. (Now that you've presented a topic, your reader may be asking, "So what?" Here is the place to briefly state the implications or applications.)

6. Bibliography/Reference Lists/Footnotes

Check with your instructor for the rules that govern this part of your paper.

B. ROUGH DRAFTS

Your writing starts with a rough draft. Try writing the rough draft of a short paper in one sitting or in a single day. Don't worry too much about the details of style, punctuation, or smooth transitions from one point to the next. Just put down the main points. If you get stuck on a section, skip it and come back to it later. Worrying too much about the mechanics of form and style at this stage may discourage you — you may even decide you can't write. Your first draft is a diamond in the rough. You add the polish later.

Double-space what you write — it's easier to read and, if it's on paper, easier to make corrections and insert things. If you use only one side of the paper, you can "cut and paste" — that is, move sections around to different places like you can with a word processor.

C. ADDITIONAL DRAFTS AND THE FINAL PRODUCT

1. Give yourself some time between drafts so you can then have a fresh look at what you've written.

2. As you read each paragraph, check that it has a clear focus, says something relevant, and is correctly placed in the manuscript.

3. On your final draft, pay close attention to sentence structure, spelling, punctuation, etc. Check with your instructor for special writing rules.

4. Always proofread your final product before handing it in. More marks are lost from simple mechanical errors than any other single reason. Some proofreaders read manuscripts backwards to catch spelling errors easily missed when reading for meaning. And never rely on the "spell check" option on your computer. You still need to read your work over carefully.

5. Check with your instructor for the correct style to use for footnotes.

6. Check with your instructor about the use of headings or subtitles in your essay.

VIII. SOME GENERAL TIPS ON INCREASING WRITING SKILLS

1. Writing requires practice. Many accomplished authors write every day and seldom for more than a few hours a day.

2. Set aside 30 minutes each day to write something (letters, notes, summaries of your reading material, a diary, etc.).

3. If you have trouble finding anything to say or putting it into words, talk with family members or fellow students. Tell them what you're working on and then explain it to them. Some students even record their conversations so they'll remember how they said it.

4. Look for examples showing the style and format your assignment should take. For instance, to write up a report of an experiment, look at professional journals to see how it can be done. Ask your instructor for a sample. Librarians are another good source of information.

5. Some writers "dictate," using a recorder to put their thoughts into words and speed up the process. You might try this method.

6. After your paper is written, check each paragraph for the focus and perspective (see Section 3: Reading and Remembering).

7. Always type your papers or use a word processor. Some instructors are very particular about the style and format of written assignments, so make sure you know what the instructor expects.

8. Let friends or family members read your paper and then "quiz" them to make sure they understand what you're trying to say.

9. Before you produce your final product, let the paper sit for a few days, and then read it again.

10. When your paper is marked and returned, note the instructor's corrections and comments for your next paper.

11. Remember that almost everything in print has been read and rewritten several times before going off to the printer.

12. The ideal essay-writing schedule for the well-organized person would be:

    • on the day the assignment is given — brainstorm

    • within two days — make the general outline and do more brainstorming

    • within one week — get started on the research

    • two weeks before the essay is due — prepare the final outline and rough draft (try to write the rough draft in one sitting)

    • three days before the essay is due — complete the final product

    • due date — proofread and hand in

13. When you're given an assignment, spend time carefully reading the instructions.

IX. ACTION WORDS FOR WRITING ESSAYS AND REPORTS

A few basic action words can indicate what you're doing with the topic of your essay or report. You may be "describing" the life history of the cattle tick; you may be "evaluating" the impact of price controls; or you may be "analyzing" an author's method of building a plot to a crisis. Of course, some topics should be treated in more than one way. For instance, you may wish to "describe" and "evaluate" a two-party political system. When deciding how to treat a topic, go over the following action words and select one or two that reflect what you'll be doing with your topic.

A. EVALUATE (to assess the worth of something)

1. To judge something's worth, determine its use, goal, idea, and so on.

2. Make a value judgment(s) about something.

3. List reasons for that judgment.

4. Develop examples, evidence, contrasts, and details that support your judgment and clarify your reasoning.

B. DISCUSS (usually to give the pros and cons of some assertion, quotation, policy, etc.)

1. List the pros (for) and cons (against) of what is being asserted.

2. Develop details, examples, and the like to support or clarify each pro and con.

3. Based on your lists, conclude with your view of what is being asserted.

C. COMPARE AND CONTRAST (to give the similarities and differences of two or more objects, subjects, stories, theories, etc.)

1. List bases (criteria) for comparing and contrasting.

2. For each basis, judge similarities and differences.

3. Provide details and examples to support and clarify your judgment.

4. Assess overall similarities or differences.

5. Determine the significance of the similarities and differences, considering the purpose of the comparison.

D. ANALYZE (to break into parts)

1. Break the subject of the essay (a process, procedure, object, etc.) into its major parts.

2. Connect and write about the parts according to the purpose of the question: describe, explain, criticize, etc.

E. CRITICIZE (to judge the good and bad points of something)

1. List good points and bad points.

2. Develop details, examples, contrasts, etc. to support judgments.

3. Make overall judgments of quality.

F. EXPLAIN (to show the causes of or reasons for something)

1. In science, usually show the sequence of events that produces a result, thoroughly presenting the details of each step.

2. In the humanities and often in the social sciences, list factors that influence an action, developing evidence for each factor's potential influence.

G. DESCRIBE (to give the major features of something)

1. List reasons for a position on something.

2. List reasons against another position on something.

3. Refute possible objections to your arguments.

4. Expand on reasons, objections, and replies with details, examples, consequences, logical connections, and so on.

H. COMMENT (to make statements about something)

What you do depends on what the comment calls for — a position, a discussion, an explanation, a judgment, an evaluation, etc. The meaning of "comment" is determined largely by the context within which it occurs.

I. DEMONSTRATE (to show something)

How you show a point depends on the nature of the subject matter. You might provide evidence, clarify the logical basis for something, appeal to principles or laws as in an explanation, or simply supply a range of opinion and examples.

X. HOW-TO-WRITE-AN-ESSAY BOOKS REFERENCES B

Please refer to Section 6 on page 137 for a bibliography of books that discuss writing style, format, and the preparation of papers and reports.

5
Consolidating Your Learning and Preparing for Exams

Survey Your Present Learning and Remembering Habits

		Always	Almost Always	Usually	Sometimes	Almost Never	Never
1	I find it easy to concentrate when I study.						
2	I set specific goals each time I study.						
3	I deal well with information overload.						
4	I reorganize information into outlines, tables, etc. when I prepare for exams.						
5	I remember information I study.						
6	I use at least 50% of my study time to recall, recite and output information.						
7	I share my knowledge by participating in a study group.						
8	I perform up to my potential on exams.						
9	I quiz myself to prepare for exams.						
10	I practice relaxation methods to help me cope with anxiety.						

If you answered "always" or "almost always" to most of these survey items, you may want to skim over this section. Otherwise, read over the information and try the exercises.

I. LEARNING

A. HOW DO YOU LEARN?

Before working through this section, here are a few more questions to answer. Your answers will help you relate what is discussed here to your own learning experiences.

- How do I make the transition from reading, listening, or doing something to actually learning it?

- How do I know when I've learned something?

- How do I evaluate what and how much I've learned?

- How do I deal with formal evaluation methods such as exams and essays?

- What experiences do I have with exams? Have they been successful experiences?

This section provides you with some information on:

> General principles of learning
> Strategies for remembering
> Techniques for consolidating your learning
> Techniques for preparing for and writing exams and papers

B. WHY DO WE LEARN?

To answer this question, we need to look at some of the results of learning. In general, we learn because it benefits or rewards us in some way. Write down some of the ways you benefit by learning something (your rewards) here:

_____

_____

_____

_____

_____

_____

Do the rewards you listed fall into these categories?

- To meet formal requirements — that is, a grade, mark, diploma, etc.

- Self-satisfaction: a) increased self-esteem, and b) more personal information

- Application in daily life: a) in family and social circles, b) in your job, c) to seek advancement, and d) for leisure or self-development

You may have other answers as well.

C. SETTING LEARNING GOALS

Look again at the list of rewards for learning. For every major learning project you take on, ask yourself, How will I be rewarded for learning it?

When you're satisfied there is a benefit, the next step is to set your learning goals. To do this, answer the following questions.

1. What do I need to do to achieve the reward I want?

    For instance, if you were an English teacher who wanted to become department head, taking a distance education math course might not lead to a promotion, but taking a course in administration might.

    Or, if you wanted to develop your math skills to allow you to take advanced courses in math and science, then mastering fundamental math principles would serve your goal.

2. How much of the material/information do I want to learn?

    Do you want to know every detail in a chapter, or just the main ideas? Do you see how this relates back to determining our purpose in reading (page 36).

3. How long do I want to retain the learned material? Do I want it just to get me through an exam, or will I be using it for other reasons?

Your answers will affect how you study and review material and how you consolidate your learning. They will also determine how you use the suggestions in this section. As you work through the material in this section, you'll be developing more effective ways of learning and integrating information. Keep these questions and your answers in mind.

We'll now look at one of the principles of learning and see how it can be applied.

II. PRACTICE: THE FIRST PRINCIPLE OF LEARNING AND REMEMBERING

A. HOW MUCH CAN WE LEARN AND REMEMBER?

Are there times when you find that, no matter what you do, you just can't concentrate? Halfway through a lecture or a chapter, do you suddenly realize you can't remember anything you've heard or read? If so, you've experienced "limited processing capacity." In other words, there are limits to how much you can learn at one time. For instance, during the first few hours of a day-long workshop, you might be excited and alert, but by late afternoon, you're tired and unable to concentrate. At this point, you're likely "overloaded." How does this happen? Do you remember the example of the flow diagram in the Reading and Remembering section?

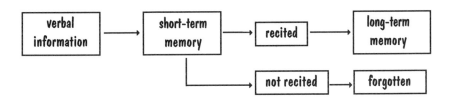

Our short-term memory is limited in terms of how much new information it can handle at a time. This limit is 5 to 9 items (7+/-2). When more than 9 new units of information — a new concept, a mathematical formula, a specific detail — enter, overload results and some information gets pushed out. So if a chapter you're reading introduces too many new concepts (e.g., more than 9), continuing to read may do nothing but confuse and frustrate you. In other words, you'll be overloaded.

B. WHAT TO DO ABOUT OVERLOAD

When this happens to you, you need to get those new concepts from your short-term memory into your long-term memory. Your long-term memory is almost infinite in its capacity.

Although it's useless to keep reading after you're overloaded, that's probably often what you try to do. But what you really need to do is stop and do something to get the information into your long-term memory.

"Rehearsal," "recital" or "practice" is essential for getting information into your long-term memory. This is something you can easily do. It includes anything that involves actually using the new concept, word, idea, or formula. It may be as simple as looking up a new word in the dictionary, or spending an hour trying to understand why a mathematical formula works. It may mean discussing a concept with someone or, better yet, trying to explain it. Or it may be any number of other methods you use to understand something. Once you understand the material, you can then return to your reading until you reach the overload point again. More on this later.

1. Practice Actions

The principle of practice is based upon the observation that we learn by doing things. It is, of course, essential to "input" information we want to learn — through experience, reading, listening, and observing — but it's also essential to "output" the information to improve our ability to remember and perform. Studies have shown that by practicing output activities, our ability to retain verbal information can be increased several times.

But what kind of practice is best? It depends on what you want to learn to do. If you want to do well on the course exam, the best type of practice is writing exams. If the course exam will be made up of essay questions, practice writing answers to appropriate essay questions. If it's a multiple-choice exam, practice answering multiple-choice questions.

In the same way, if your learning goal is to be able to talk about, or apply, or analyze, or judge the information you study, the best practice is doing these things. Practice what you will be asked to do.

Surprisingly few students apply this "practice" principle to their academic studies. Even though most students would never consider learning to play an instrument or use a computer without lots of practice, not many practice gaining knowledge and critical thinking skills.

 Exercise 1: Identifying Practice Activities
(20 minutes)

Reflect for a moment on a course you're taking or are about to take. What do you expect to learn to do in the course? What will you be required to do for an exam, during class sessions, or on assignments?

Here are a few actions to consider:

> **writing** about the subject matter
> **talking** about the subject matter
> **recalling** facts, formulae, etc.
> **drawing** graphs, figures, or illustrations
> **defining** terms, principles, or concepts
> **solving** problems
> **selecting** phrases that complete sentences
> **matching** concepts
> **determining** the truth of statements
> **analyzing** concepts, procedures, or methods
> **demonstrating** an action or procedure
> **judging** the quality of information
> **comparing** or **contrasting** points of view or theories

Now, for your course, list some things you'll be asked to do.

_____

_____

_____

_____

_____

_____

_____

Did you consider exams, reports, term papers, and assignments?

Did you think beyond the course to situations where you might apply your learning?

Check this list from time to time to see if you're practicing the relevant activities for your course.

_____

2. Practice Conditions

Clearly, learning is improved if you practice what you want to be able to do. But it's improved even more if you practice under the same kinds of conditions you'll experience when you write exams, give an in-class presentation, and so on.

Think about an upcoming exam situation. What will be available to you during the exam? Books? Calculator? Notes? TV? If you won't have it during the exam, then practice exam activities without it.

Even the time of day can be important. If your exam will be from 9:00 a.m. to 12:00 noon, practice for the exam during a comparable three-hour period.

The more alike your practice and test situations, the better. Of course, practice under any set of conditions is better than no practice at all.

III. ORGANIZATION: THE SECOND PRINCIPLE OF LEARNING AND REMEMBERING

Let's return to the problem of information overload — and some good news about it. You can increase the amount you absorb into your short-term memory! Although we can only hold about 7 units of new information at a time, each of those can hold a number of subunits of material. For instance, the word "cat" is just one unit of information, but think about all the information you hold about that one unit. You know what a cat looks like, sounds like, behaves like, and so on. "Cat" is a cue word for all your information about cats.

We can apply what we know about short-term memory to learning and, more specifically, to the concept of organization. Suppose you want to learn this list of words. See how many you can remember after one reading. Then, without looking, write them on a piece of paper from memory.

blender	scissors	pants
sock	machete	saw
bowl	dress	hat
shoe	knife	paper cutter
cookie sheet	spoon	frying pan

You probably couldn't remember more than 7 of these 15 seemingly unrelated items after a first reading. Now, look at them after they've been organized into three categories.

Cooking Equipment	Wearing Apparel	Cutting Instruments
blender	shoe	scissors
bowl	sock	machete
cookie sheet	dress	knife
spoon	pants	saw
frying pan	hat	paper cutter

Are they easier to recall when there are only three different groups, each with 5 items in it? Organized this way, you can handle a much larger number of items because the group headings serve as cue words.

How does this relate to your studying? There are two main ways.

Reading. As you read or review, look for categories and groups of information or concepts. When you look through your notes, try grouping together similar items. Review will be much easier if you concentrate on the larger groups, not the smaller details. Work on the details later (see Section 3: Reading and Remembering).

Goal Setting. When you schedule your study time and set your goals for each hour, remember your "limited processing capacity." An unrealistic goal will only leave you feeling frustrated when you become overloaded and can't do as much as you planned.

As you study and read for the next few days, try to determine your "overload" point. At that point, stop and use the principles of practice and organization to get the information you have absorbed into your long-term memory before moving on.

IV. APPLYING PRINCIPLES TO CONSOLIDATE LEARNING

There are four ways of practicing or "rehearsing" what you've learned. Use these to prepare for a formal evaluation of your learning (such as an exam). You can also apply these principles in other areas of your life.

A. PRACTICE BY SHARING THE INFORMATION

If you've ever taught or explained something to someone, afterward you may have found that you understood the material better yourself. This is one of the best ways to practice what you've learned. If you can't find someone to teach, discuss the new information with someone or form a study group with some of your classmates. A study group is not only an effective way to review, but it can also be a lot more fun than working on your own. If you can't be part of a study group, ask a friend to let you explain the material to him/her. Be creative. Some students use a tape recorder or even their pet as a listener.

Using study groups is a popular way to help learning. Here are some practical tips to follow when forming one.

1. There should be three to five people in the group. Pick a chairperson to keep things on track and to make sure everyone participates actively.

2. Everyone must do individual study and preparation before the group meets. The group time can then be used for practice, discussion, and consolidation of learning.

3. The group should meet regularly, perhaps two hours a week.

4. Always have a set agenda. For example:

    a. Business arising from the last meeting (e.g., solutions to unsolved problems, corrections, etc.)

    b. Overview of the session's topic (e.g., each member gives a two-minute overview of the point he/she sees as most important)

    c. Practice exam (e.g., each person brings several questions and everyone writes out answers under exam conditions)

    d. Discussion of practice exam questions and answers (e.g., members read the question they asked, say what a complete answer would include, and the group discusses their answers)

    e. Preview of the next week's readings, etc.

    f. Set agenda for next meeting

    g. Socialize

5. Each member should participate in and contribute to the session.

B. USING ORGANIZATIONAL PATTERNS

Remember the different ways of organizing notes we discussed in Part V of Section 3: Reading and Remembering? Now is your chance to go over all the material or notes you've collected on a topic or chapter to see how the ideas fit together into a meaningful whole. Experiment with different organizational patterns by getting a large piece of paper and seeing how many ways you can rearrange the information. Just the process of organizing something often helps you remember it. This chapter from an abnormal psychology text has been organized in two different ways.

EARLY HISTORY OF ABNORMALITY

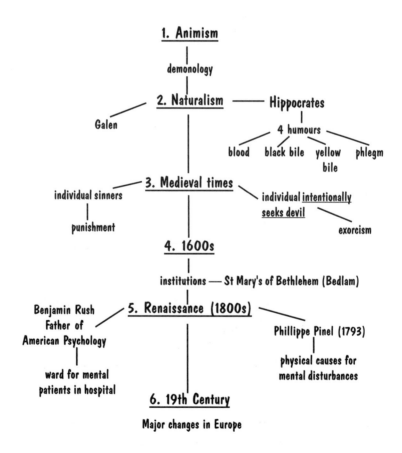

Don't worry if this doesn't make much sense to you. Review notes are often only meaningful to the person who wrote them.

Another way of organizing the same notes is to use a standard outline.

Early History of Abnormality

I.   Animism
     A. demonology   What does this mean?

II. Naturalism
     A. Galen   What did Galen do?
     B. Hippocrates
         1.   4 humours
              a)   blood
              b)   black bile
              c)   yellow bile
              d)   phlegm

III. Medieval Times
     A. Individual as sinner
         1.   treatment = punishment
     B. Individual intentionally seeks devil
         1.   treatment = exorcism by priests

IV. 1600s
     A. First institutions — St. Mary's of Bethlehem (Bedlam)

V.   Renaissance
     A. Phillippe Pinel   Who was Pinel?
     B. Benjamin Rush
         1.   physical causes for mental disturbances
         2.   treatment = hospitalization

VI. 19th Century
     A. Major changes   What were these major
                                     changes?

Note: The questions indicate areas where more information is necessary. When these questions are answered, the notes for review will be complete.

C. Remembering Techniques

Although organizing your notes, reading actively, and listening well will usually be all you need to do to learn the material, at times you'll need to memorize specific details.

There are two ways of trying to memorize material. One is "rote memory," where you simply repeat to yourself what you want to learn until you remember it. It's not much fun, though, and it's very hard work. The other way is to use "mnemonic devices" (memory aids), which are fun to use and really help. Generally, a mnemonic is a way of associating something unfamiliar with something familiar — that is, taking something you want to remember and associating it with something you know well. There are seven main types of mnemonic devices.

1. The Method of Loci

This method is quite simple to use and is based on the fact that our visual memory can enhance our verbal memory. To use it, imagine a familiar sequence of locations (loci = locations). For example, you might imagine walking from your bedroom through the house and into the kitchen. As you imagine, visualize as vividly as possible a fixed sequence of locations (bedroom door, hall closet, painting in the hall, living room couch, TV, ...). Practice this familiar sequence until you can "walk through it" without missing a single location. Now that you know this sequence of locations, you can associate items you want to learn with it.

Consider the example of a shopping list with the following items to remember: carrots, celery, pork chops, margarine, and flour. Now imagine your living room, and take a mental walk around it. There's a chandelier on the ceiling, a palm growing in the corner, a magazine rack by the couch, a coffee table, and a vase.

Now let your imagination run wild. Hanging tastefully from the chandelier is a bunch of carrots. That palm in the corner is really a gracefully swaying stalk of celery. The magazine rack holds neat rows of pork chops, and next to it is the coffee table glistening with margarine. A final touch is the "flour" vase.

When you get to the grocery store, picture your living room. All those images will jump out at you, and you'll remember your shopping list. But don't do it out loud. You'll get very strange looks!

Exercise 2: Using the Method of Loci
(15 minutes)

1. Imagine a familiar sequence of locations as described above.

2. Select a list of items that you need to learn in your course (e.g., the titles of Shakespeare's plays, the noble gases, the sequence of events leading up to a significant historical event, etc.)

3. Now, at your own pace and as vividly and concretely as possible, visualize the list items as part of your sequence of locations.

4. Practice recalling the list by mentally "walking through" the sequence and "seeing" your list of items.

---

2. Analogies

Describing a heart as a pump or saying that the tubes in the lung are branched like a fruit tree are examples of analogies. Analogies can be based on similarities of function (heart and pump) or form (lung tubes and tree branches).

3. Idiosyncratic Relations

When you're trying to remember what a word means, look for something in the word that you can associate with its meaning. For instance, consider the difference between port and starboard. "Left" has fewer letters than "right" and "port" has fewer letters than "starboard." Therefore, port = left and starboard = right. What color of light is on the port side? Well, port is a red wine, so the light on the port side must be red. Idiosyncratic relations work best for small lists that you frequently mix up.

4. Rhymes

If you're creative, you can make a poem out of almost everything. Remember:

> I before E except after C
> and when it says "ay" as in
> "neighbor" and "weigh"

> or

> Thirty days hath September
> April, June, and November ...

5. Doodling

You learned about doodling in Section 3 (page 66). It really works for some people, and remember, the sillier your doodle, the more likely you are to remember it.

6. Key Words

If you need to remember several concepts or ideas, pick out one key word from each idea and remember that. You'll be surprised at how easily you can then remember the whole idea.

Try this the next time you listen to the news. For each news story, pick one significant word and write it down. When the news is over, see how many of the stories you can retell by using these key words.

7. Acrostics

An acrostic is usually a group of words in which the first letter of each word stands for something you want to memorize. If, for instance, you wanted to remember a biological classification system, you would remember:

Kings	=	**K**ingdom
play	=	**p**hylum
cards	=	**c**lass
on	=	**o**rder
fairly	=	**f**amily
good	=	**g**enus
soft	=	**s**pecies
velvet	=	**v**ariety

You can easily adapt mnemonic devices to your own learning style. If you're a visual person, then analogies, the method of loci, or doodling may be best for you. If you prefer listening, rhymes and acrostics may work better. Experiment and see which remembering techniques help you the most.

D. BOOKS ON MEMORY TECHNIQUES REFERENCES C

If you want to learn more about techniques that improve memory, refer to Section 6, page 138 for some good sources of information.

V. PREPARING FOR AND WRITING EXAMS

A. WHY HAVE EXAMS?

Exams are not given to trick you, to make you anxious, or to satisfy some hidden need of the instructor. In fact, the principle reasons for exams are:

- to give you a chance to put together all the relevant information, to sort out the main ideas, and to do things — define, solve, analyze — that are relevant to the course (see Exercise 1, page 117). Exam questions often ask for practical applications of a theory or ask you to compare and contrast some major themes, concepts, or issues. Questions like these help you fit your knowledge together.

- to let you see if you've learned and if you can remember the material you've studied.

- to motivate your studying by providing a concrete reason for doing it. And feedback from exams rewards studying and learning.

- to provide the instructor with a method of evaluating students' learning and, therefore, her/his teaching. If the whole class fails an exam, the instructor must be doing something wrong.

B. REVIEWING FOR EXAMS

The review/rehearsal methods for preparing for exams have already been discussed. Here are some more hints.

1. Make a detailed list of every topic you need to know for your exam (from textbooks, extra readings, films, and lectures).

2. Number the topics on your list in order of importance, and concentrate on the high-priority items.

3. If you haven't already done so, put together your textbook notes, lecture notes, and any other notes you have, by topic.

4. Reorganize and regroup your notes for each topic in a concise, thorough, meaningful, and organized manner. The process of doing this will help you learn.

5. If your exam is likely to be subjective (essay questions), choose four or five of your highest-priority topics and study these in depth. Try writing short essays on the most important topics, giving yourself 30 to 60 minutes for each essay (a typical amount of time in an exam situation).

6. Note anything your instructor emphasized and pay particular attention to this material.

7. Make up your own questions and answer them.

8. Write old exams for practice. (Ask your instructor for some.)

9. Memorize essential details or formulae.

C. STUDY CARDS

Using study (or "flash") cards is another way to improve your learning, your memory, and your exam performance. This is a good method to use for courses that involve learning large numbers of definitions, formulae, concepts, and principles.

Study cards are basically self-tests — you can quiz yourself and then check your answers. Once you've organized what you need to know for a section of the course (a chapter, several lectures, etc.), make study cards to cover this information.

Use a 3- x 5-inch index card (or a small piece of paper). On one side, write a key term, a partial formula, or a question. On the other side, write a definition, an example, the full formula, or a short answer.

A sample study card prepared for a course in human learning follows.

Question

```
(Side A)
Four characteristics
of short-term memory?
```

Answer

```
(Side B)
1. limited capacity: 7+/- 2
2. short duration: 20 sec
3. susceptible to "overload"
4. susceptible to interference
```

This example is from a course in economics.

```
(Side A)

Divisions of Economics
```

```
(Side B)
1. Macroeconomics
2. Microeconomics
        1. Demand
        2. Supply
        3. Distribution
```

Study Card Tips

1. Don't put too much information on a study card. Remember the "7+/-2" rule.

2. Look at one side and try to recall the other side without looking. Then, check your answer.

3. Use the cards both ways — use Side A to recall Side B and vice versa.

4. Shuffle the cards frequently to practice remembering the material in different orders.

5. Set aside a card you remember easily and just look at it once in a while. If you keep forgetting a card's information, rewrite the card — break the information down into smaller parts and use several cards.

6. Carry your study cards with you so you can test yourself often.

7. Swap cards with members of your study group, if you have one.

D. WRITING EXAMS

1. Subjective Exams (Essays and Paragraphs)

- Read the directions and skim the whole exam first. Do you have all of the exam? How many questions do you have to answer?

- Decide how much time to spend on each question depending on how much it's worth. And be sure to leave yourself some time to read things over when you're finished writing. For example, for a three-hour (180-minute) exam that has three essay questions worth 20 points each and one essay worth 40 points, you could spend ½ hour on each 20-point question, 1 hour on the 40-point question, and ½ hour on planning and review.

- Underline key words in the directions. Make sure you understand what's required. If it says, "Do three out of five questions," underline <u>three out of five</u>, so you don't get mixed up and do all five.

- Read each question several times to be absolutely sure you understand what you're being asked and what you need to include in your answer.

- Make a brief outline for each question. Check the questions and outlines to make sure they match. Use brainstorming (see Section 4).

- Use your outline to write out the answer for each question.

- Keep your answers concise and to the point.

- Check your answers for spelling, punctuation, grammar, etc.

2. **Objective Exams (Multiple Choice, Short Answer, True/False, Matching)**

- Answer the easiest questions first; then, go back to the ones you left.

- On a multiple-choice question, read the question carefully and try to remember the answer before you look at the possible answers.

- Answer all the questions unless it says not to guess. In general, if you can narrow your choices (from four to two, for instance), it's better to guess, even if you might lose marks.

If you get your exams back, go over them to see where you did well and where you went wrong. You can learn a lot from mistakes. And remember, writing exams is a skill that you'll get better at with practice.

VI. COPING WITH STRESS

Those pre-exam jitters can actually be positive — they can make you more alert and add some incentive to do well. If you're well prepared, though, you likely won't feel too much anxiety.

But sometimes before a really important exam, even the best-prepared student can get worried and fearful of going "blank." It's important to be able to recognize the symptoms of anxiety and to know what to do about them.

These symptoms fall into two main groups.

A. WORRY SYMPTOMS

Doubts and negative thoughts make up these symptoms. For example, "I know I'm going to fail this exam" or "I never do well in exams" or "I'll never remember anything" are typical thoughts.

As soon as you find yourself thinking these thoughts, ask yourself why you feel that way. Have you ever failed an exam before? Did you study hard for it? How do you know you'll never remember anything? If you've learned something well, there's no reason you should forget it when the exam comes along.

It's hard to deal with and change these negative thoughts, but it's worth trying. Tell yourself positive things instead, like "I'm going to do well on this exam because I really know and understand the material" or "I can do this" or "I'm a good student."

B. PHYSIOLOGICAL SYMPTOMS

These take different forms in different people, but can include sleeplessness, headaches, stomachaches, and tenseness. Relaxation is the key here.

Try doing some slow deep-breathing, concentrating on relaxing the various muscles of your body. A few deep breaths just before starting your exam will help. And, while you relax, imagine yourself doing something well. Some people find that it helps to get out and do some vigorous physical exercise when they get tense. Try it if you have pre-exam jitters! It will certainly take your mind off your exam! Start practicing these things well before you need them. Don't wait until just before an exam.

 Exercise 3: Learning to Relax (20 minutes)

We are all born with a "relaxation response," which we tend to lose as we get older and become involved in the stresses of everyday life. This exercise is designed to help you relearn this response and reexperience the feeling of relaxation.

Once each day, choose a 20-minute time period when you're free of distractions and interruptions (the phone, TV, etc.) and at least two hours after eating. Or, you can do this exercise when you go to bed each night.

1. Sit quietly in a comfortable position.

2. Let your eyes close.

3. Take three or four deep, deep breaths. Inhale slowly and feel the tension and pressure in your chest. As you breathe out, silently tell yourself to relax. Resume natural breathing for 30 seconds between each deep breath.

4. Now breathe easily and naturally, but continue to tell yourself to relax as you exhale each breath. Focus your attention on your breathing and allow it to happen naturally. Continue this for 5 minutes.

5. As you continue this natural breathing, tense, then slowly relax the muscles of your body. Start at your toes. Tense them, then let them relax, feeling the tension ooze out. Slowly work your way up your legs, through your abdomen, up through your arms and chest, to your neck and head. Tense, then relax one muscle group at a time. Allow a minute of relaxation between each muscle group.

6. Enjoy the quiet feelings of relaxation. Notice how your different muscle groups feel. Relax them a bit more. Remain quiet for another 5 minutes.

Don't worry if you didn't relax this first time, and don't try to force yourself to relax. With practice, it will come naturally and effortlessly. And the more you practice, the easier it will be to relax. (The results will be better, too.)

By practicing daily, you'll soon be skilled enough in this technique to calm yourself and cope with stressful situations. When you're under stress, close your eyes and allow yourself to relax.

VII. CONCLUSION

Now that you have a good basic knowledge of some fundamental study skills, you can decide how to apply these skills to your own learning situation.

But there's a big difference between knowing about study skills and actually using them. So, use the skills that work for you and, most importantly, make them a part of your everyday study routine. That's how you'll become a more efficient and effective learner.

6
References

BOOKS ON FINANCIAL AID AND PLANNING

Collins, Charles. *College Orientation — Education for Relevance* Massachusetts: Holbrook Press Inc., 1969, chapters 3 & 12.

Ellis, David. *Becoming a Master Student*. South Dakota: College Survival Inc., 1991, chapter 10.

Farrar, Ronald. *College 101*. New Jersey: Peterson's Guides Inc., 1984, chapters 6 & 7.

Gardener, John and Jewler, Jerome. *College is only the Beginning*. California: Wadsworth Publishing Co., 1989, chapter 21.

Gibbs, Keith. *University Degrees and Learning With Ease*. Ontario: Keith J. Gibbs, 1993, chapter 6.

Hofmann Nemiroff, Greta. *Transitions: Succeeding in College and University*. Ontario: Harcourt Brace & Co., 1994, chapter 2.

Pivar, William. *The Whole Earth Textbook*. Ontario: W.B. Saunders Co., 1978, chapters 8 & 10.

BOOKS ON PROFESSORS

Butler, John and Jacoby, Theresa. *Higher Grades through Better Notes*. California: Fearon Publishers, 1965.

Elliot, Chandler. *The Effective Student*. New York: Harper and Row Publishers, 1966, chapter 3.

Farrar, Ronald. *College 101*. New Jersey: Peterson's Guides Inc., 1984.

Gardener, John and Jewler, Jerome. *College is only the Beginning*. California: Wadsworth Publishing, Co., 1989.

Semones, James. *Effective Study Skills*. Florida: Holt, Rinehart & Winston, Inc., 1991.

Walter, Timothy L. and Siebert, A.L. *Student Success*. Florida: Holt, Rinehart & Winston, Inc., 1993.

BOOKS ON CONCEPT MAPPING

Bellanca, James. *The Cooperative Think Tank*. Illinois: Skylight Publishing, 1990, chapter 5.

Buzan, Tony. *The Mind Mapping Book*. England: BBC Publications, 1993.

Buzan, Tony. *Use your Head*. England: BBC Publications, 1974, chapter 4.

Good, Steve and Jensen, Bill. *The Students Only Survival Guide to Essay Writing*. British Columbia: Orca Book Publishers, 1995.

Kesselman-Turkel, Judi and Peterson, Franklynn. *Study Smarts*. Illinois: Contemporary Books Inc., 1981, chapter 9.

Pauk, Walter. *How to Study in College*. Massachusetts: Houghton Mifflin Co., 1989, chapters 3 & 10.

Smith, Samuel, Shores, Louis and Brittain, Robert. *Best Methods of Study*. New York: Barnes and Noble Inc., 1955, chapter 16.

Sotiriou, Peter. *Integrating College Study Skills*. California: Wadsworth Inc., 1989, chapter 11.

BOOKS ON MOTIVATION

Fleet, Joan and Reaume, Denise. *Power Over Time*. Ontario: Harcourt Brace & Co., 1994, chapters 5 & 6.

Gibbs, Keith. *University Degrees and Learning with Ease*. Ontario: Keith J. Gibbs, 1993, chapter 1.

Hofmann Nemiroff, Greta. *Transitions: Succeeding in College and University*. Ontario: Harcourt Brace & Co., 1984, chapter 6.

Quaintance, William. *Learning to Learn*. Maine: J. Weston Walch Publishers, 1976.

BOOKS ON MEMORY

Albrecht, Karl. *Brain Power*. New York: Prentice Hall Inc., 1980, chapter 12.

Buzan, Tony. *Use your Head*. England: BBC Publications, 1974, chapter 3.

Ellis, David. *Becoming a Master Student*. South Dakota: College Survival Inc., 1991, chapter 3.

Higbee, K.L. *Your Memory*. New Jersey: Prentice Hall Inc., 1977.

Hunter, I.M.L. *Memory*. England: Penguin Books Ltd., 1968.

Larayne, Harry and Lucas, Terry. *The Memory Book*. New York, 1974.

New York State Personnel and Guidance Association. *Tips to Improve Personal Study Skills*. New York: Delmar Publishers, 1968, chapter 6.

Pauk, Walter. *How to Study in College*. Massachusetts: Houghton Mifflin Co., 1989.

Semones, James K. *Effective Study Skills*. Florida: Holt, Rinehart & Winston, Inc., 1991.

University of Victoria. *Strategies for Studying*. British Columbia: Division of University Extensions, 1996.

BOOKS ON PROBLEM-SOLVING TECHNIQUES

Elliot, Chandler. *The Effective Student*. New York: Harper and Row Publishers, 1966, chapter 3.

Polya, G. *How to Solve It*. New Jersey: Princeton University Press, 1973.

Samson, Richard. *Problem Solving Improvement*. New York: McGraw Hill Book Co., 1970.

Taylor, Catherine, Avery, Heather and Strath, Lucille. *Making Your Mark*. Ontario: Harcourt Brace & Co., 1994.

BOOKS ON STRESS/ANXIETY

Farrar, Ronald. *College 101*. New Jersey: Peterson's Guides Inc., 1984.

Fleet, Joan and Reaume, Denise. *Power Over Time — Student Success with Time Management*. Ontario: Harcourt Brace & Co., 1994, chapter 7.

Gardener, John and Jewler, Jerome. *College is only the Beginning*. California: Wadsworth Publishing, Co., 1989.

Gibbs, Keith. *University Degrees and Learning with Ease*. Ontario: Keith J. Gibbs, 1993, chapter 7.

Grassick, Patrick. *Making the Grade*. Ontario: Macmillan of Canada, 1983, chapter 3.

Hofmann Nemiroff, Greta. *Transitions: Succeeding in College and University*. Ontario: Harcourt, Brace & Co., 1994.

Pauk, Walter. *How to Study in College*. Massachusetts: Houghton Mifflin Co., 1989, chapter 2.

Pivar, William. *The Whole Earth Textbook*. Ontario: W.B. Saunders Co., 1978, chapter 9.

Semones, James. *Effective Study Skills*. Florida: Holt, Rinehart & Winston, Inc., 1991.

Tobias, Sheila. *Overcoming Math Anxiety*. Massachusetts: Houghton Mifflin Co., 1980, chapter 8.

Walter, Timothy and Siebert, A.L. *Student Success*. Florida: Holt, Rinehart & Winston, Inc., 1993.

BOOKS ON THINKING PROCESSES

Albrecht, Karl. *Brain Power*. New York: Prentice Hall Inc., 1980.

Barrass, Robert. *Students Must Write*. New York: Methuen and Co., 1982, chapter 5.

Bellanca, James. *The Cooperative Think Tank*. Illinois: Skylight Publishing, 1990.

Ellis, David. *Becoming a Master Student*. South Dakota: College Survival Inc., 1991, chapter 7.

Hofmann Nemiroff, Greta. *Transitions: Succeeding in College and University*. Ontario: Harcourt Brace & Co., 1994, chapter 5.

Maiorana, Victor. *How to Learn and Study in College*. New Jersey: Prentice Hall Inc., 1980, chapters 6 & 7.

Semones, James. *Effective Study Skills*. Florida: Holt, Rinehart & Winston, Inc., 1991.

BOOKS ON TIME MANAGEMENT

Brown, Thomas. *Study: Where, When & How*. Newfoundland: Harper-Row Publishers, 1970.

Buzan, Tony. *Use your Head*. England: BBC Publications, 1974.

Ellis, David. *Becoming a Master Student*. South Dakota: College Survival Inc., 1991.

Farrar, Ronald. *College 101*. New Jersey: Peterson's Guides Inc., 1984, chapter 2.

Fleet, Joan and Reaume, Denise. *Power over Time*. Ontario: Harcourt Brace & Co., 1994.

Gibbs, Keith. *University Degrees and Learning with Ease*. Ontario: Keith J. Gibbs, 1993, chapter 5.

Maiorana, Victor. *How to Learn and Study in College*. New Jersey: Prentice Hall Inc., 1980, chapters 3 & 4.

McGee-Cooper, Ann and Trammell, Duane. *Time Management for Unmanageable People*. New York: Bantam Books, 1994.

New York State Personnel and Guidance Association. *Tips to Improve Personal Study Skills*. New York: Delmar Publishers, 1968.

Pauk, Walter. *How to Study in College*. Massachusetts: Houghton Mifflin, Co., 1989.

Rowntree, Derek. *Learn How to Study*. England: Hazell, Watson and Viney Ltd., 1970.

Semones, James. *Effective Study Skills*. Florida: Holt, Rinehart & Winston, Inc., 1991

Sotiriou, Peter. *Integrating College Study Skills*. California: Wadsworth Inc., 1989.

University of Victoria. *Strategies for Studying*. British Columbia: Division of University Extensions, 1996.

Walter, Timothy and Siebert, A.L. *Student Success*. Florida: Holt, Rinehart & Winston, Inc., 1993.

BOOKS ON STUDY TIPS AND TECHNIQUES

Bellanca, James. *The Cooperative Think Tank*. Illinois: Skylight Publishing, 1990.

Brown, Thomas. *Study: Where, When & How*. Newfoundland: Harper and Row Publishers, 1970, chapter 3.

Burkhardt, Diana & Rutherford, Des. *Study Skills in Mathematics*. England: Shell Centre For Math Education, University of Nottingham, 1981.

Butler, John and Jacoby, Theresa. *Higher Grades Through Better Notes*. California: Fearon Publishers, 1965.

Elliot, H. Chandler. *The Effective Student*. New York: Harper and Row Publishers, 1966, chapters 1 & 2.

Farrar, Ronald. *College 101*. New Jersey: Peterson's Guides Inc., 1984, chapter 2.

Gardener, John and Jewler, Jerome. *College is only the Beginning*. California: Wadsworth Publishing Co., 1989, chapter 4.

Gibbs, Keith. *University Degrees and Learning with Ease*. Ontario: Keith J. Gibbs, 1993, chapter 2.

Good, Steve and Jensen, Bill. *The Students Only Survival Guide to Essay Writing*. British Columbia: Orca Book Publishers, 1995.

Hofmann Nemiroff, Greta. *Transitions: Succeeding in College and University*. Ontario: Harcourt Brace & Co., 1994, chapter 5.

Kesselman-Turkel, Judi and Peterson, Franklynn. *Study Smarts*. Illinois: Contemporary Books Inc., 1981.

Pauk, Walter. *How to Study in College*. Massachusetts: Houghton Mifflin Co., 1989, chapters 4 & 11.

Pivar, William. *The Whole Earth Textbook*. Ontario: W.B. Saunders Co., 1978, chapter 5.

Quaintance, William. *Learning to Learn*. Maine: T. Weston Walch Publishers, 1976.

Rowntree, Derek. *Learn How to Study*. England: Hazell, Watson & Viney Ltd., 1970, chapters 1 & 2.

Semones, James. *Effective Study Skills*. Florida: Holt, Rinehart & Winston, Inc., 1991

Smith, Samuel, Shores, Louis and Brittain, Robert. *Best Methods of Study*. New York: Barnes and Noble Inc., 1955.

Sotiriou, Peter. *Integrating College Study Skills*. California: Wadsworth Inc., 1989, chapter 12.

Staton, Thomas. *How to Study*. Alabama: Thomas F. Staton, 1968.

Taylor, Catherine, Avery, Heather and Strath, Lucille. *Making your Mark*. Ontario: Harcourt Brace & Co., 1994, chapter 2.

University of Victoria. *Strategies for Studying*. British Columbia: Division of University Extensions, 1996.

BOOKS ON TAKING EFFECTIVE NOTES

Barrass, Robert. *Students Must Write*. New York: Methuen and Co., 1982, chapter 2.

Butler, John and Jacoby, Theresa. *Higher Grades through Better Notes*. California: Fearon Publishers, 1965.

Buzan, Tony. *Use your Head*. England: BBC Publications, 1974, chapter 4.

Elliot, Chandler. *The Effective Student*. New York, Harper and Row Publishers, 1966, chapter 3.

Ellis, David. *Becoming a Master Student*. South Dakota: College Survival Inc., 1991, chapter 5.

Gibbs, Graham. *Teaching Students to Learn*. England: Open University Press, 1981, chapter 2.

Good, Steve and Jensen, Bill. *The Students Only Survival Guide to Essay Writing*. British Columbia: Orca Book Publishers, 1995.

Hofmann Nemiroff, Greta. *Transitions: Succeeding in College and University*. Ontario: Harcourt Brace and Co., 1994.

Kesselman-Turkel, Judi and Peterson, Franklynn. *Note Taking Made Easy*. Illinois: Contemporary Books Inc., 1982.

New York State Personnel and Guidance Association. *Tips to Improve Personal Study Skills*. New York: Delmar Publishers, 1968, chapter 5.

Pauk, Walter. *How to Study in College*. Massachusetts: Houghton Mifflin Co., 1989, chapter 3.

Rowntree, Derek. *Learn How to Study*. England: Hazell, Watson and Viney Ltd., 1970, chapter 6.

Semones, James. *Effective Study Skills*. Florida: Holt, Rinehart & Winston, Inc., 1991.

Smith, Samuel, Shores, Louis and Brittain, Robert. *Best Methods of Study*. New York: Barnes and Noble Inc., 1955, chapter 4.

Sotiriou, Peter. *Integrating College Study Skills*. California: Wadsworth Inc., 1989, chapter 3.

University of Victoria. *Strategies for Studying*. British Columbia: Division of University Extensions, 1996.

BOOKS ON WRITING SKILLS/PAPERS

Barrass, Robert. *Students Must Write*. New York: Methuen and Co., 1982.

Barret, Blair. *Paragraph Patterns*. New York: McGraw Hill Book Co., 1970.

Buckley, Janne. *Fit to Print*. Ontario: Harcourt Brace & Co., 1991.

Dawe, Alan, Watson, Wendy and Harrison, David. *Assessing English Skills: Writing*. British Columbia. Ministry of Education, 1984.

Gibbs, Graham. *Teaching Students to Learn*. England: Open University Press, 1981, chapter 2.

Gibbs, Keith. *University Degrees and Learning with Ease*. Ontario: Keith J. Gibbs, 1993, chapter 3.

Good, Steve and Jensen, Bill. *The Students Only Survival Guide to Essay Writing*. British Columbia: Orca Book Publishers, 1995.

Gordon, Burgard, Young. *A Programmed Approach to Writing*. Ontario: Ginn and Co., 1964.

Harrison et al. *Notes on the Preparation of Essays in the Arts and Sciences*. Ontario: Academic Skills Centre, 1985.

Kesselman-Turkel, Judi and Peterson, Franklynn. *Research Shortcuts*. Illinois: Contemporary Books Inc., 1982.

Kesselman-Turkel, Judi and Peterson, Franklynn. *The Grammar Crammer*. Illinois: Contemporary Books Inc., 1982.

Kesselman-Turkel, Judi and Peterson, Franklynn. *Getting it Down*. Illinois: Contemporary Books Inc., 1983.

Messenger, William and De Bruyn, Jan. *The Canadian Writer's Handbook*. Ontario: Prentice Hall Inc., 1986.

Hofmann Nemiroff, Greta. *Transitions: Succeeding in College and University*. Ontario: Harcourt Brace and Co., 1994.

New York State Personnel and Guidance Association. *Tips to Improve Personal Study Skills*. New York. Delmar Publishers, 1968, chapter 4.

Pearlman, Daniel and Paula. *Guide to Rapid Revision*. New York: Odyssey Press, Inc., 1965.

Pivar, William. *The Whole Earth Textbook*. Ontario. W.B. Saunders Co., 1978, chapter 7.

Robertson, Hugh. *The Research Essay*. Ontario: Piperhill Publications, 1991.

Ross-Larson, Bruce. *Edit Yourself*. New York: W.W. Norton and Co., 1982.

Rowntree, Derek. *Learn how to Study*. England: Hazell, Watson and Viney Ltd., 1970.

Semones, James. *Effective Study Skills*. Florida: Holt, Rinehart & Winston, Inc., 1991.

Smith, Samuel, Shores, Louis and Brittain, Robert. *Best Methods of Study*. New York: Barnes and Noble Inc., 1955.

Sotiriou, Peter. *Integrating College Study Skills*. California: Wadsworth Publishing Co., 1989.

Taylor et al. *Thinking it Thru*. Ontario: Academic Skills Centre, 1987.

University of Victoria. *Strategies for Studying*. British Columbia: Division of University Extensions, 1996.

Walter, Timothy and Siebert, A.L. *Student Success*. Florida: Holt, Rinehart & Winston, Inc., 1993.

Witty, Paul. *How you can be a Better Student*. New York: Sterling Publishing Co., 1957, chapter 2.

BOOKS ON SPELLING

Dawe, Alan, Watson, Wendy and Harrison, David. *Assessing English Skills: Writing*. British Columbia: Ministry of Education, 1984, chapter 7.

Dixon, Robert. *The Surefire Way to Better Spelling*. New York: St. Martin's Press, 1993.

Kesselman-Turkel, Judi and Peterson, Franklynn. *Spelling Simplified*. Illinois: Contemporary Books Inc., 1983.

Messenger, William and De Bruyn, Jan. *The Canadian Writer's Handbook*. Ontario: Prentice Hall Inc., 1986, chapter 6.

BOOKS ON MATH SKILLS

Burkhardt, Diana and Rutherford, Des. *Study Skills in Mathematics*. England: Shell Centre for Math Education, University of Nottingham, 1981.

Ellis, David. *Becoming a Master Student*. South Dakota: College Survival Inc., 1991, chapter 6.

Kenna, L.A. *Understanding Mathematics with Visual Aids*. New Jersey: Littlefield Adams & Co., 1993.

Maiorana, Victor. *How to Learn and Study in College*. New Jersey: Prentice Hall Inc., 1980, chapter 16.

Meyer, Jerome. *Fun with Mathematics*. New York: Premier Books, 1961.

Tobias, Sheila. *Overcoming Math Anxiety*. Massachusetts: Houghton Mifflin Co., 1980.

BOOKS ON RESOURCE/REFERENCE TECHNIQUES

Barrass, Robert. *Students Must Write*. New York: Methuen and Co., 1982.

Dawe, Alan, Watson, Wendy and Harrison, David. *Assessing English Skills: Writing*. British Columbia: Ministry of Education, 1984, chapter 2.

Ellis, David. *Becoming a Master Student*. South Dakota: College Survival Inc., 1991, chapter 4.

Good, Steve and Jensen, Bill. *The Students Only Survival Guide to Essay Writing*. British Columbia: Orca Book Publishers, 1995.

Kesselman-Turkel, Judi and Peterson, Franklynn. *Research Shortcuts*. Illinois: Contemporary Books Inc., 1982, chapter 3.

New York State Personnel and Guidance Association. *Tips to Improve Personal Study Skills*. New York: Delmar Publishers, 1968, chapter 7.

Robertson, Hugh. *The Research Essay*. Ontario: Piperhill Publications, 1991.

Semones, James. *Effective Etudy Skills*. Florida: Holt, Rinehart & Winston, Inc., 1991, chapter 8.

Smith, Samuel, Shores, Louis and Brittain, Robert. *Best Methods of Study*. New York: Barnes and Noble Inc., 1955, chapter 8.

BOOKS ON ORAL EXAMS AND SPEECHES

Elliot, H. Chandler. *The Effective Student*. New York: Harper and Row Publishers, 1966, chapter 18.

Grassick, Patrick. *Making the Grade*. Ontario: Macmillan of Canada, 1983.

Lorayne, Harry and Lucas, Terry. *The Memory Book*. New York: Ballantine Books, 1974, chapter 6.

Lieb, Anthony. *Speaking for Success*. Ontario: Harcourt Brace and Co., 1993.

Maiorana, Victor. *How to Learn and Study in College*. New Jersey: Prentice Hall Inc., 1980.

BOOKS ON EXAM PREPARATION

Brown, Thomas. *Study: Where, When & How*. Newfoundland: Harper and Row Publishers, 1970, chapter 4.

Butler, John and Jacoby, Theresa. *Higher Grades through Better Notes*. California: Fearon Publishers, Inc., 1965, chapters 3 & 4.

Ellis, David. *Becoming a Master Student*. South Dakota: College Survival Inc., 1991, chapter 6.

Farrar, Ronald. *College 101*. New Jersey: Peterson's Guides Inc., 1984, chapter 2.

Grassick, Patrick. *Making the Grade*. Ontario: Macmillan of Canada, 1983, chapter 1.

Hofmann Nemiroff, Greta. *Transitions: Succeeding in College and University*. Ontario: Harcourt, Brace and Co., 1994, chapter 5.

New York State Personnel and Guidance Association. *Tips to Improve Personal Study Skills*. New York: Delmar Publishers, 1968, chapter 4.

Pauk, Walter. *How to Study in College*. Massachusetts: Houghton Mifflin Co., 1989, chapters 4 & 11.

Rowntree, Derek. *Learn How to Study*. England: Hazell, Watson and Viney Ltd., 1970, chapter 7.

Semones, James. *Effective Study Skills*. Florida: Holt, Rinehart & Winston, Inc., 1991, chapters 3 & 14.

Staton, Thomas. *How to Study*. Alabama: Thomas F. Staton, 1968, chapter 6.

Taylor, Catherine. Avery, Heather and Strath, Lucille. *Making your Mark*. Ontario: Harcourt, Brace & Co., 1994.

University of Victoria. *Strategies for Studying*. British Coliumbia: Division of University Extensions, 1996, chapter 5.

BOOKS ON TAKING EXAMS

Butler, John and Jacoby, Theresa. *Higher Grades through Better Notes*. California: Fearon Publishers, 1965, page 77.

Elliot, Chandler. *The Effective Student*. New York: Harper and Row Publishers, 1966, chapter 3.

Ellis, David. *Becoming a Master Student*. South Dakota: College Survival Inc., 1991, chapter 6.

Gibbs, Graham. *Teaching Students to Learn*. England: Open University Press., 1981, chapter 2.

Gibbs, Keith. *University Degrees and Learning with Ease*. Ontario: Keith J. Gibbs, 1993, chapter 3.

Grassick, Peter. *Making the Grade*. Ontario: Macmillan of Canada, 1983, chapters 2 & 3.

Maiorana, Victor. *How to Learn and Study in College*. New Jersey: Prentice Hall Inc., 1980, chapter 19.

New York State Personnel and Guidance Association. *Tips to Improve Personal Study Skills*. New York: Delmar Publishers, 1968, chapter 4.

Pauk, Walter. *How to Study in College*. Massachusetts: Houghton Mifflin Co., 1989.

Pivar, William. *The Whole Earth Textbook*. Ontario: W.B. Saunders Co., 1978, chapter 6.

Rowntree, Derek. *Learn How to Study*. England: Hazell, Watson and Viney Ltd., 1970, chapter 7.

Sotiriou, Peter. *Integrating College Study Skills*. California: Wadsworth Publishing Co., 1989, chapters 14 & 15.

Staton, Thomas. *How to Study*. Alabama: Thomas F. Staton, 1968.

Taylor, Catherine, Avery, Heather and Strath, Lucille. *Making your Mark*. Ontario: Harcourt Brace and Co., 1994, chapter 3.

Witty, Paul. *How you can be a Better Student*. New York: Sterling Publishing Co., 1957, chapter 2.

BOOKS ON LISTENING SKILLS

Elliot, H. Chandler. *The Effective Student*. New York: Harper and Row Publishers, 1966, chapters 1 & 3.

Nichols, Ralph. *The Complete Course in Listening*. New York: Dun and Bradstreet Inc., 1971.

Pauk, Walter. *How to Study in College*. Massachusetts: Houghton Mifflin Co., 1989, chapters 3 & 6.

Sotiriou, Peter. *Integrating College Study Skills*. California: Wadsworth Publishing Co., 1989, chapter 2.

Staton, Thomas. *How to Study*. Alabama: Thomas F. Staton, 1968.

BOOKS ON LEARNING FOREIGN LANGUAGES

Lorayne, Harry and Lucas, Terry. *The Memory Book*. New York: Ballantine Books, 1974, chapter 7.

Pauk, Walter. *How to Study in College*. Massachusetts: Houghton Mifflin Co., 1989, chapter 20.

Smith, Samuel, Shores, Louis and Brittain, Robert. *Best Methods of Study*. New York: Barnes and Noble Inc., 1955

OTHER BOOKS STUDENTS MIGHT FIND USEFUL

Atkinson, Rhonda and Longman, Debbie Guice. *Reading Enhancement and Development, 5th edition*. Minnesota: West Publishing Co., 1955.

Atkinson, Rhonda and Longman, Debbie Guice. *Vocabulary for College and Beyond*. Minnesota: West Publishing Co., 1990.

Atkinson, Rhonda and Longman, Debbie Guice. *Getting Oriented*. Minnesota: West Publishing Co., 1995.

Atkinson, Rhonda and Longman, Debbie Guice. *College Learning and Study Skills, 3rd edition*. Minnesota: West Publishing Co., 1993.

Good, Steve and Jensen, Bill. *The Students Only Survival Guide to Essay Writing*. British Columbia: Orca Book Publishers, 1995.

Ross-Larsen, Bruce. *Edit Yourself: A Manual for Everyone who Works with Words*. New York: W.W. Norton Co., 1996.

Robinson, Adam and staff of the Princeton Review. *Word Smart*. Ontario: Villard Books, 1992.

Robinson, Adam and staff of the Princeton Review. *Word Smart II*. Ontario: Villard Books, 1993.

Freedman, Michael. *Word Smart, Genius Edition*. Ontario: Villard Books, 1995.

Staff of the Princeton Review. *Grammar Smart*. Ontario: Villard Books, 1993.

Schaffzin, Nicholas Reid. *Reading Smart*. Ontario: Villard Books, 1994.

Pauk, Walter. *How to Study in College, 5th edition*. Massachusetts: Houghton Mifflin Co., 1993.

Bensel-Meyers, L. *Rhetoric for Academic Reasoning*. New York: HarperCollins Publishers Inc., 1992

Davis, Martha and Eshelman, Elizabeth Robbins. *The Relaxation and Stress Reduction Workbook, 3rd Edition*. California: New Harbinger Publications, 1988.

Kanar, Carol. *The Confident Student, 2nd Edition*. Massachusetts: Houghton Mifflin Co., 1995.

Eberts, Marjorie and Gisler, Margaret. *How to Prepare for College*. Illinois: VGM Career Horizons, 1990.

Berg, Howard Stephen. *Super Reading Secrets*. New York: Warner Books, 1992.

Meyer, Russell and Mylan, Sheryl. *An Integrated Approach to Reading and Writing*. New York: St. Martin's Press Inc., 1995.

Tarshis, Barry. *Grammar for Smart People*. New York: Pocket Books, 1992.

Bosworth, Stefan and Brisk, Marion. *Learning Skills for the Science Student*. Minnesota: West Publishing Co., 1994.

Deem, James. *Study Skills in Practice*. Massachusetts: Houghton Mifflin Co., 1993.

Deese, James and Deese, Ellin. *How to Study and Other Skills for Success in College*. New York: McGraw Hill Book Co., 1994.

Adetumbi, Moses. *You're a Better Student Than you Think*. Alabama: Adex Book Co., 1992.

Chaffee, John. *The Thinker's Guide to College Success*. Massachusetts: Houghton Mifflin Co., 1995.

Sonbuchner, Gail Murphy. *Help Yourself: How to take Advantage of your Learning Styles*. New York: New Readers Press, 1991.

Chafetz, Michael. *Smart for Life: How to Improve your Brain Power at any Age*. New York: Penguin, 1992.

Cortina, Joe, Elder, Janet and Gonnet, Katherine. *Comprehending College Textbooks: Steps to Understanding and Remembering What you Read, 3rd Edition*. New York: McGraw Hill Book Co., 1996.

Taylor, Karen, Strath, Louise and Avery, Heather. *Clear, Correct, Creative: A Handbook for Writers of Academic Prose*. Ontario: Trent University, Academic Skills Centre, 1991.

Robinson, Adam. *What Smart Students Know: Maximum Grades, Optimum Learning, Minimum Time*. New York: Crown Trade Paperbacks, 1993.

Norton, Sarah and Green, Brian. *Essay Essentials*. Ontario: Holt, Rinehart & Winston, Ltd., 1991

Rooke, Constance. *The Clear Path: A Guide to Writing English Essays*. Ontario: Nelson Canada, 1995.

Winston, Stephanie. *Stephanie Winston's Best Organizing Tips*. New York: Fireside, 1996.

Tobias, Sheila and Tomizuka, Carl. *Breaking the Science Barrier: How to Explore and Understand the Sciences*. New York: College Entrance Examination Board, 1992.

Fry, Ron. *Take Notes*. New Jersey: Career Press Inc., 1991.

Smith, Richard Manning. *Mastering Mathematics: How to be a Great Math Student*. California: Wadsworth Publishing Co., 1991.

Nolting, Paul. *Winning at Math: Your Guide to Learning Mathematics through Successful Study Skills*. Florida: Academic Success Press, 1991.

Lobban, Christopher and Schefter, Maria. *Successful Lab Reports: A Manual for Science Students*. New York: Cambridge University Press, 1992.

Shepherd, James. *College Spelling Skills*. Massachusetts: Houghton Mifflin Co., 1996.

Covey, Stephen, Merrill, A. Roger, and Merrill, Rebecca. *First Things First*. New York: Simon and Schuster, 1994.

Ruggiero, Vincent Ryan. *Becoming a Critical Thinker, 2nd Edition*. Massachusetts: Houghton Mifflin Co., 1996.

Fleet, Joan and Reaume, Denise. *Power Over Time: Student Success with Time Management*. Ontario: Harcourt Brace and Co., 1994.

Leib, Anthony. *Speaking for Success: The Canadian Guide*. Ontario: Harcourt Brace and Co., 1993.

Coman, Marcia and Heavers, Kathy. *How to Improve your Study Skills*. Illinois: NTC Publishing Group, 1990.

Wong, Linda. *Essential Study Skills*. Massachusetts: Houghton Mifflin Co., 1994.

Northey, Margot. *Making Sense: A Student's Guide to Research Writing and Style*. Ontario: Oxford University Press Canada, 1993.

Gaidosch, Bernie. *Common Sense: A Short Guide to Essay Writing*. Ontario: Harcourt Brace & Co., 1994

Ferrett, Sharon. *Peak Performance*. Illinois: Richard D. Irwin Inc., 1994.

Fleet, Joan, Goodchild, Fiona and Zajchowski, Richard. *Skills and Strategies for Canadian Students*. Ontario: Harcourt Brace and Co., 1990.

INTERNET ADDRESSES WITH INFORMATION THAT STUDENTS MIGHT FIND USEFUL:

http://www.coun.uvic.ca/learn/learn.htm (University of Victoria Counselling Services)

http://coos.dartmouth.edu/~gmz/asctr.html#study (Dartmouth College) http://www.ucc.vt.edu/stdysk/stdyhlp.html (Virginia Tech)

http://www.mindtools.com/

http://www.nolimits.com/nolimits/buzhome.html (Tony Buzan Homepage)

http://www.utexas.edu/student/lsc/handouts.html (University of Texas)

LEARNING SKILLS VIDEOS

Gibson, Sandra and Gibson, James. *Making A's in College*. Georgia: Workbooks Press, 1994.

Olney, Claude W. *Where There's a Will There's an A*. Pennsylvania: Chesterbrook Educational Publishers, 1988.

Science Study Skills. Nova Scotia: Mount Saint Vincent University, 1991.

Thayer, Kathy. *Time Management*. Indiana: Purdue University Liberal Arts Learning Centre, 1993.

Thayer, Kathy. *How Do I Show What I Know?* Indiana: Purdue University Liberal Arts Learning Centre, 1993.

Thayer, Kathy. *How Do I Know What to Study?* Indiana: Purdue University Liberal Arts Learning Centre, 1993.

Thayer, Kathy. *Lecture Notetaking*. Indiana: Purdue University Liberal Arts Learning Centre, 1993.